FREE Test Taking Tips DVD Offer

To help us better serve you, we have developed a Test Taking Tips DVD that we would like to give you for <u>FREE</u>. **This DVD covers world-class test taking tips that you can use to be even more successful when you are taking your test.**

All that we ask is that you email us your feedback about your study guide. Please let us know what you thought about it — whether that is good, bad or indifferent.

To get your **FREE Test Taking Tips DVD**, email <u>freedvd@studyguideteam.com</u> with "FREE Test Taking Tips DVD" in the subject line and the following information in the body of the email:

    a.   The title of your study guide.

    b.   Your product rating on a scale of 1-5, with 5 being the highest rating.

    c.   Your feedback about the study guide. What did you think of it?

    d.   Your full name and shipping address to send your free DVD.

If you have any questions or concerns, please don't hesitate to contact us at <u>freedvd@studyguideteam.com</u>.

Thanks again!

EMT Basic Exam Textbook

Table of Contents

Quick Overview

As you draw closer to taking your exam, preparing becomes more and more important. Thankfully, you have this study guide to help you get ready. Use this guide to help keep your studying on track and refer to it often.

This study guide contains several key sections that will help you be successful on your exam. The guide contains tips for what you should do the night before and the day of the test. Also included are test-taking tips. Knowing the right information is not always enough. Many well-prepared test takers struggle with exams. These tips will help equip you to accurately read, assess, and answer test questions.

A large part of the guide is devoted to showing you what content to expect on the exam and to helping you better understand that content. Near the end of this guide is a practice test so that you can see how well you have grasped the content. Then, answers explanations are provided so that you can understand why you missed certain questions.

Don't try to cram the night before you take your exam. This is not a wise strategy for a few reasons. First, your retention of the information will be low. Your time would be better used by reviewing information you already know rather than trying to learn lots of new information. Second, you will likely become stressed as you try to gain large amount of knowledge in a short amount of time. Third, you will be depriving yourself of sleep. So be sure to go to bed at a reasonable time the night before. Being well-rested helps you focus and remain calm.

Be sure to eat a substantial breakfast the morning of the exam. If you are taking the exam in the afternoon, be sure to have a good lunch as well. Being hungry is distracting and can make it difficult to focus. You have hopefully spent lots of time preparing for the exam. Don't let an empty stomach get in the way of success!

When travelling to the testing center, leave earlier than needed. That way, you have a buffer in case you experience any delays. This will help you remain calm and will keep you from missing your appointment time at the testing center.

Be sure to pace yourself during the exam. Don't try to rush through the exam. There is no need to risk performing poorly on the exam just so you can leave the testing center early. Allow yourself to use all of the allotted time if needed.

Remain positive while taking the exam even if you feel like you are performing poorly. Thinking about the content you should have mastered will not help you perform better on the exam.

Once the exam is complete, take some time to relax. Even if you feel that you need to take the exam again, you will be well served by some down time before you begin studying again. It's often easier to convince yourself to study if you know that it will come with a reward!

Test-Taking Strategies

1. Predicting the Answer

When you feel confident in your preparation for a multiple-choice test, try predicting the answer before reading the answer choices. This is especially useful on questions that test objective factual knowledge or that ask you to fill in a blank. By predicting the answer before reading the available choices, you eliminate the possibility that you will be distracted or led astray by an incorrect answer choice. You will feel much more confident in your selection if you read the question, predict the answer, and then find your prediction among the answer choices. After using this strategy, be sure to still read all of the answer choices carefully and completely. If you feel unprepared, you should not attempt to predict the answers. This would be a waste of time and an opportunity for your mind to wander in the wrong direction.

2. Reading the Whole Question

Too often, test takers scan a multiple-choice question, recognize a few familiar words, and immediately jump to the answer choices. Test authors are aware of this common impatience, and they will sometimes prey upon it. For instance, a test author might subtly turn the question into a negative, or he or she might redirect the focus of the question right at the end. The only way to avoid falling into these traps is to read the entirety of the question carefully before reading the answer choices.

3. Looking for Wrong Answers

Long and complicated multiple-choice questions can be intimidating. One way to simplify a difficult multiple-choice question is to eliminate all of the answer choices that are clearly wrong. In most sets of answers, there will be at least one selection that can be dismissed right away. If the test is administered on paper, the test taker could draw a line through it to indicate that it may be ignored; otherwise, the test taker will have to perform this operation mentally or on scratch paper. In either case, once the obviously incorrect answers have been eliminated, the remaining choices may be considered. Sometimes identifying the clearly wrong answers will give the test taker some information about the correct answer. For instance, if one of the remaining answer choices is a direct opposite of one of the eliminated answer choices, it may well be the correct answer. The opposite of obviously wrong is obviously right! Of course, this is not always the case. Some answers are obviously incorrect simply because they are irrelevant to the question being asked. Still, identifying and eliminating some incorrect answer choices is a good way to simplify a multiple-choice question.

4. Don't Overanalyze

Anxious test takers often overanalyze questions. When you are nervous, your brain will often run wild causing you to make associations and discover clues that don't actually exist. If you feel that this may be a problem for you, do whatever you can to slow down during the test. Try taking a deep breath or counting to ten. As you read and consider the question, restrict yourself to the particular words used by the author. Avoid thought tangents about what the author *really* meant, or what he or she was *trying* to say. The only things that matter on a multiple-choice test are the words that are actually in the question. You must avoid reading too much into a multiple-choice question, or supposing that the writer meant something other than what he or she wrote.

5. No Need for Panic

It is wise to learn as many strategies as possible before taking a multiple-choice test, but it is likely that you will come across a few questions for which you simply don't know the answer. In this situation, avoid panicking. Because most multiple-choice tests include dozens of questions, the relative value of a single wrong answer is small. Moreover, your failure on one question has no effect on your success elsewhere on the test. As much as possible, you should compartmentalize each question on a multiple-choice test. In other words, you should not allow your feelings about one question to affect your success on the others. When you find a question that you either don't understand or don't know how to answer, just take a deep breath and do your best. Read the entire question slowly and carefully. Try rephrasing the question a couple of different ways. Then, read all of the answer choices carefully. After eliminating obviously wrong answers, make a selection and move on to the next question.

6. Confusing Answer Choices

When working on a difficult multiple-choice question, there may be a tendency to focus on the answer choices that are the easiest to understand. Many people, whether consciously or not, gravitate to the answer choices that require the least concentration, knowledge, and memory. This is a mistake. When you come across an answer choice that is confusing, you need to give it extra attention. A question might be confusing because you do not know the subject matter to which it refers. If this is the case, don't eliminate the answer before you have affirmatively settled on another. When you come across an answer choice of this type, set it aside as you look at the remaining choices. If you can confidently assert that one of the other choices is correct, you can leave the confusing answer aside. Otherwise, you will need to take a moment to try to better understand the confusing answer choice. Rephrasing is one way to tease out the sense of a confusing answer choice.

7. Your First Instinct

Many people struggle with multiple-choice tests because they overthink the questions. If you have studied sufficiently for the test, you should be prepared to trust your first instinct once you have carefully and completely read the question and all of the answer choices. There is a great deal of research to suggest that the mind can come to the correct conclusion very quickly once it has obtained all of the relevant information. At times, it may seem to you as if your intuition is working faster even than your reasoning mind. This may in fact be true. The knowledge you obtain while studying may be retrieved from your subconscious before you have a chance to work out the associations that support it. Verify your instinct by working out the reasons that it should be trusted.

8. Key Words

Many test takers struggle with multiple-choice questions because they have poor reading comprehension skills. Quickly reading and understanding a multiple-choice question requires a mixture of skill and experience. To help with this, try jotting down a few key words and phrases on a piece of scrap paper. Doing this concentrates the process of reading and forces the mind to weigh the relative importance of the question's parts. In selecting words and phrases to write down, the test taker thinks about the question more deeply and carefully. This is especially true for multiple-choice questions that are preceded by a long prompt.

9. Subtle Negatives

One of the oldest tricks in the multiple-choice test writer's book is to subtly reverse the meaning of a question with a word like *not* or *except*. If you are not paying attention to each word in the question, you can easily be led astray by this trick. For instance, a common question format is, "Which of the following is...?" Obviously, if the question instead is, "Which of the following is not....?," then the answer will be quite different. Even worse, the test makers are aware of the potential for this mistake and will include one answer choice that would be correct if the question were not negated or reversed. A test taker who misses the reversal will find what he or she believes to be a correct answer and will be so confident that he or she will fail to reread the question and discover the original error. The only way to avoid this is to practice a wide variety of multiple-choice questions and to pay close attention to each and every word.

10. Reading Every Answer Choice

It may seem obvious, but you should always read every one of the answer choices! Too many test takers fall into the habit of scanning the question and assuming that they understand the question because they recognize a few key words. From there, they pick the first answer choice that answers the question they believe they have read. Test takers who read all of the answer choices might discover that one of the latter answer choices is actually *more* correct. Moreover, reading all of the answer choices can remind you of facts related to the question that can help you arrive at the correct answer. Sometimes, a misstatement or incorrect detail in one of the latter answer choices will trigger your memory of the subject and will enable you to find the right answer. Failing to read all of the answer choices is like not reading all of the items on a restaurant menu. You might miss out on the perfect choice.

11. Spot the Hedges

One of the keys to success on multiple-choice tests is paying close attention to every word. This is never more true than with words like *almost, most, some,* and *sometimes*. These words are called "hedges", because they indicate that a statement is not totally true or not true in every place and time. An absolute statement will contain no hedges, but in many subjects, like literature and history, the answers are not always straightforward. There are always exceptions to the rules in these subjects. For this reason, you should favor those multiple-choice questions that contain hedging language. The presence of qualifying words indicates that the author is taking special care with his or her words, which is certainly important when composing the right answer. After all, there are many ways to be wrong, but there is only one way to be right! For this reason, it is wise when taking a multiple-choice test to avoid answers that are absolute. An absolute answer is one that says things are either all one way or all another. They often include words like *every, always, best,* and *never*. If you are taking a multiple-choice test in a subject that doesn't lend itself to absolute answers, be on your guard if you see any of these words.

12. Long Answers

In many subject areas, the answers are not simple. As already mentioned, the right answer often requires hedges. Another common feature of the answers to a complex or subjective question are qualifying clauses, which are groups of words that subtly modify the meaning of the sentence. If the question or answer choice describes a rule to which there are exceptions or the subject matter is complicated, ambiguous, or confusing, the correct answer will require many words in order to be expressed clearly and accurately. In essence, you should not be deterred by answer choices that seem excessively long. Oftentimes, the author of the text will not be able to write the correct answer without offering some qualifications and modifications. As a test taker, your job is to read the answer choices thoroughly and completely and to select the one that most accurately and precisely answers the question.

13. Restating to Understand

Sometimes, a question on a multiple-choice test is difficult not because of what it asks but because of how it is written. If this is the case, restate the question or answer choice in different words. This process serves a couple of important purposes. First, it forces you to concentrate on the core of the question. In order to rephrase the question accurately, you have to understand it well. Rephrasing the question will concentrate your mind on the key words and ideas. Second, it will present the information to your mind in a fresh way. This process may trigger your memory of some useful scrap of information picked up while studying.

14. True Statements

Sometimes an answer choice will be true in itself, but it does not answer the question. This is one of the main reasons why it is essential to read the question carefully and completely before proceeding to the answer choices. Too often, test takers skip ahead to the answer choices and look for true statements. Having found one of these, they are content to select it without reference to the question above. Obviously, this provides an easy way for test makers to play tricks. The savvy test taker will always read the entire question before turning to the answer choices. Then, having settled on a correct answer choice, he or she will refer to the original question and ensure that the selected answer is relevant. The mistake of choosing a correct-but-irrelevant answer choice is especially common on questions related to specific pieces of objective knowledge, like historical or scientific facts. A prepared test taker will have a wealth of factual knowledge at his or her disposal, but may be careless in its application.

15. No Patterns

One of the more dangerous ideas that circulate about multiple-choice tests is that the correct answers tend to fall into patterns. These erroneous ideas range from a belief that B and C are the most common right answers, to the idea that an unprepared test-taker should answer "A-B-A-C-A-D-A-B-A." It cannot be emphasized enough that pattern-seeking of this type is exactly the WRONG way to approach a multiple-choice test. To begin with, it is highly unlikely that the test maker will plot the correct answers according to some predetermined pattern. The questions are scrambled and delivered in a random order. Furthermore, even if the test maker was following a pattern in the assignation of correct answers, there is no reason why the test maker would know which pattern he or she was using. Any attempt to discern a pattern in the answer choices is a waste of time and a distraction from the real work of taking the test. A test taker would be much better served by extra preparation before the test than by reliance on a pattern in the answers.

Medical, Legal, and Ethical

First responders, EMT-B and EMT-I

First responders: 40 hours of training in CPR and dealing with breathing emergencies, bleeding, administering oxygen and the use of AED. First responders are generally those first on the scene, such as police officers and firefighters.

EMT-B: 110 hours of training in CPR and BLS plus training to transport patients. They are trained to do patient assessments, administer CPR, use the AED, immobilize fractures, upper airway adjuncts, spinal immobilization, deal with bleeding and shock as well as assist with oxygen and breathing. They are also trained to use common emergency equipment that is found in an ambulance. They have practical training in an emergency room or ambulance. EMT-I: 200 to 400 hours of training. In addition to the training of an EMT-B, they are able to administer intravenous therapy, perform orotracheal intubation, and interpret cardiac rhythms and defibrillations.

Ryan White Law

The Ryan White Law was created in 1990 and put into practice in 1994. The law states that all EMS, fire and law enforcement agencies have a designated infection control officer to manage issues of exposure. This officer will be trained in the law and have an educated understanding of communicable diseases. They are responsible for the management of situations where exposure to communicable diseases is involved. This includes assisting the exposed individual(s) (employee) in receiving medical follow-up. This officer is also responsible for receiving and communicating information regarding exposure. This law protects the EMT by requiring all exposure to be communicated.

Universal precautions

Universal Precautions are a set of recommendation defined by the Center of Disease Control to prevent the transmission of HIV and other blood born pathogens in a health care setting. The recommendations are:
- Use of protective barriers such as gloves, gowns and masks.
- Avoid needle pokes and injuries from other equipment such as scalpels by practicing safe handling techniques and using puncture proof containers for disposal.
- Areas exposed to blood or other body fluids should be washed immediately; hands should be washed after degloving.
- Avoid mouth-to-mouth contact by having ventilation aids available for resuscitation.
- Any health care workers with lesions or sores should avoid patient contact until healed

BSI precautions

Body substance isolation (BSI) precautions should be part of an EMT's exposure control plan and include four points:
1. Wear gloves and eye protection.
2. Wear mask and gown if possible.
3. Wash hands properly and thoroughly.
4. Dispose of sharps carefully and safely.

These precautions assume that all body fluids are potentially infectious, whereas the Center for Disease Control precautions distinguishes certain bodily fluids as being infectious. The BSI precautions are more general and less encompassing than the universal precautions.

"Duty to act"

If an EMT suspects a patient may be infectious, they should exercise the BSI precautions and continue to provide care. To deny a person care may have legal ramifications such as neglect, breach of duty or abandonment. If a patient appears violent or there is a potential for violence within the scene, an EMT is not expected to place him or herself at risk and should call for appropriate assistance. Police are the ones with the authority to secure a crime scene and should be left to do this duty. Since this is not within the EMT scope of practice, it is not considered part of the "duty to act" whereas providing emergency medical care is.

Negligence

Negligence is where a person fails to perform a duty or provide a standard of care that a person of similar training is expected to provide. The four criteria that must be met in order for negligence to have occurred are:

1. The negligent party must have been in a position where they had a "duty to act"; in other words, they were called to the scene or were working as an EMT at the time. An off duty EMT may not be negligent.
2. "Breach of duty" occurs: the EMT did not provide the standard of care expected.
3. Damage occurred that could include anything physical or psychological.
4. The damage was a direct result of the EMT not performing their duty to the standard of care expected.

NREMT

The NREMT was established in the 1970's when it was realized that the level of pre-hospital care received by patients had a significant impact on the seriousness of their injuries and their mortality rate.

The National Registry of Emergency Medical Technicians provides a national standard for emergency medical personnel. Certification with the NREMT ensures that these personnel have met established competencies as well as educational and skill requirements. The certification process includes meeting entry requirements, completing the application process, passing practical and theoretical exams and regular renewal or recertifying procedures in order to maintain a level of competency that is consistent. The NREMT does not issue a license to practice; that is state jurisdiction.

Important abbreviations

AED (Automated External Defibrillator): Device used to detect and correct irregular cardiac rhythm by delivering an electric shock.

ALS (Advanced Life Support): Invasive life saving procedures including intravenous therapy and cardiac monitoring; mostly practiced by EMT-I but some of which is coming into the scope of EMT-B practice.

CISD (Critical Incident Stress Debriefing): Confidential meeting for EMT personnel with CISD officers and or mental health workers. The meeting is held within 24 to 72 hours of a critical incident to provide support and suggestions on how to deal with stress incurred due to the incident.

BLS (Basic Life Support): Airway, breathing and circulation (ABC): providing this through recognizing the emergency; providing artificial respiration, CPR and AED as necessary; and unblocking airway obstructions as required.

Airway

Normal breathing

Normal breathing is rhythmic and seen by a regular rise and fall of the chest. In adult breathes normally at a rate of 12 to 20 breaths per minute, a child at 15 to 30 breaths per minute and an infant at 25 to 50 breaths per minute. Breathing rate per minute is dependent on size. Normal breathing is not noisy, is even on both sides of the chest and does not require effort or use of other muscles. The depth of breath (tidal volume), which can be seen by chest movement or by feeling the movement of air at the nose and mouth, is adequate since it is not too deep or too shallow. To summarize, normal breathing can be identified by assessing rate, rhythm, quality and depth.

Physiology of breathing

As the levels of CO_2 rise in the body, the need to exhale is cued. Increased levels of CO_2 in the body cause the brain to send a signal to the breathing muscles: the diaphragm and the intercostals. The movement of these muscles expands the chest and creates negative pressure causing the lungs to expand and air to enter through the airway.

At the alveolar level are tiny capillaries where gas exchange occurs. The capillaries release CO_2 (a cellular waste product) into the alveoli and blood cells absorb oxygen which turns them the familiar bright red of arterial blood. An increase level of CO_2 in the alveolar sacs signals the body to exhale.

The anatomical components of the airway include:
1. Nose and mouth
2. Pharynx
    a. Oropharynx: Mouth cavity
    b. Nasopharynx: Nasal cavity
3. Epiglottis: Flap of skin that prevents food from entering trachea and going into the lungs at junction of esophagus and trachea
4. Cricoid Cartilage: Ring of cartilage at the lower part of the larynx
5. Larynx: Voice box
6. Trachea: The windpipe passage to the lungs; has cartilage rings
7. Bronchi: The branches of trachea that go to each lung; has cartilage rings
8. Bronchioles: Branches of the bronchi within each lung; no cartilage, can collapse
9. Alveoli: The end of the airway, where gas exchange occurs; blood is oxygenated, CO_2 is released.
10. Diaphragm: Muscle that lines the base of the thoracic cavity its contraction inflates the lungs.

Inhalation and exhalation

Inhalation is considered the active part of breathing. The diaphragm contracts by flattening out and pulling down into the abdomen; the intercostals muscles contract and open up the rib cage or thoracic cavity. Due to the increased volume inside the vacuum of the thoracic cavity, negative pressure is created, the lungs expand, and again to fill a vacuum, air flows into the lungs through the airway.

Exhalation is the passive part of breathing that happens when the muscles between the ribs (intercostals) and the diaphragm relax. The diaphragm returns to its relaxed size which brings it upward while the intercostals muscles release and the spaces between the ribs become smaller. This effectively reduces the size of the thoracic cavity, which causes the pressure to expel air from the lungs.

<u>Pediatric patient considerations</u>
Infants up to between 2 and 4 months old only breathe through their nose and are called obligate nose breathers; they haven't learned to breathe through their mouths yet.

In pediatric patients, the tongue is larger than the mouth and tends to fall back. This is often the cause of airway blockage in a non-breathing patient. The airway passage in infants and children, including the trachea, is much smaller than that of an adult. It has softer cartilage, more of it and therefore is more elastic. Because of this, obstruction can occur much easier by mucous, inflammation or ingested objects. The cricoid cartilage is the narrowest point at the base of larynx, whereas in adults the top of the larynx the narrowest point.

Rescue breathing rate for pediatric patients is 1 breath every 3 seconds. With an infant the breath is delivered as two gentle puffs from the rescuer's cheeks. Monitor for natural breathing after about ten breaths.

Open airway

An open airway is necessary for breathing; it is the first step in Emergency Medical Treatment. Breathing provides oxygen to the body tissues, by providing gas exchange at the alveoli of the lungs. Oxygen is taken in while carbon dioxide is removed. Without oxygen, tissues of the body begin to die. The heartbeat can become irregular within seconds of going without oxygen. The heart is a muscle and therefore requires oxygen to contract; the contractions of cardiac muscle constitute the heartbeat. Severe brain damage can occur after 4 to 6 minutes without oxygen.

ABC

Airway, breathing, circulation are standard in the primary assessment. Without airway there is no breathing, without breathing there is no heartbeat, without heartbeat there is no circulation.

Assessing respiration

Signs of inadequate breathing:
1. Breathing rate is less than 12 or greater than 20 breaths per minute in a healthy adult; less than 15 and greater than 30 in a child; or less than 25, greater than 50 in an infant.
2. Skin color is bright pink, red or blue.
3. Nasal flaring
4. Minimal air flow
5. Chest movement is not rhythmic; breaths are not even in volume.
6. Patient may recruit extra muscles to help in breathing; look for abdominal, neck and shoulder movement.
7. Sounds made from the airway
8. Skin is damp and clammy

By listening to breathing sounds with a stethoscope, the EMT-B can recognize certain signs of respiratory problems as well as the location of the problem. Upper airway problems can present as gurgling or snoring sounds. *Gurgling* can mean there is fluid or mucous in the upper airway. *Snoring* may be caused by partial blockage of the tongue or other obstruction. *Stridor* is a high-pitched sound coming from the upper airway during inhalation; it that may indicate blockage at the larynx. When the larynx is swollen, a lower pitched noise called *crowing* can be heard upon exhalation.

Wheezing is indicative of a lower airway problem and may be caused by asthma. When there is fluid within the alveoli of the lungs a crackling sound is heard called rales.

"Rhonchi" refers to a snoring-like sound that emits from either the upper or lower airway and is continuous. It may imply an excess of mucous in the airway.

Airway-clearing methods

Head-tilt-chin-lift maneuver
This is the basic positioning for a clear airway if the patient has no signs of head, neck or back injury. Patient should be on their back. Place palm of hand on forehead and gently apply pressure. At the same time, place the index and middle fingers under the chin and lift. This will straighten the neck and clear the airway. Check for breathing: listen, watch the chest for movement and place your cheek near the nose and mouth to feel for breath.

If there is no breathing at this point, check inside the mouth for loose dental appliances or other obvious obstructions. Try to reposition the head by repeating the head-tilt-chin-lift maneuver. If the second attempt is not successful begin rescue breathing.

Jaw thrust maneuver
The jaw thrust maneuver is used to open the airway when a head, neck or back injury is suspected. Once the patient has been determined to be unresponsive, place them in a supine position. Sit at the head of the patient, place your elbows on the surface at either side of the patient with fingers behind the angles of the jaw. Lift jaw forward. Check for breathing, open mouth to check for obstructions, such as loose dentures. If there is no breathing after attempting the jaw thrust maneuver, attempt to clear the airway using the head-tilt-chin-lift maneuver.

The jaw thrust is very difficult to do properly and can cause increase cervical spine damage if done incorrectly. Therefore, the head-tilt-chin-lift is considered the most effective technique to clear the airway.

Patients with stoma or tracheostomy
A stoma is a connection from the trachea to the surface of the skin that enables a person to breathe by passing most of the upper airway. The stoma may be cleared by suctioning if your local protocols allow for it. Mouth-to-stoma breathing using a mask is possible but may cause unnecessary exposure. Use a BVM device with a pediatric mask, covering mouth and nose to prevent air escape. If you use the BVM over the stoma, the head and neck do not need to be repositioned. Or attempt ventilation through the mouth, covering the stoma hole; this may also remove any obstruction in the airway.

Hypoxia

Hypoxia is a condition that develops when the body tissues are not receiving enough oxygen. It can be a result of inadequate breathing or shortness of breath. A patient with hypoxia may initially appear disoriented, irritable, nervous, and have a rapid pulse. Later stages will appear as labored breathing, chest pain and, in extreme cases, the patient will begin to turn blue due to lack of oxygen in the blood (cyanosis). Conditions that are associated with hypoxia are: heart attack, asthma, smoke inhalation, drug overdose, shock and fluid in the lungs.

Suctioning
Suctioning is used to clear the airway. If there is a small obstruction, suctioning may clear it. It is also used to clear mucous, blood, vomit and fluid from the airway. If a patient is making gurgling sounds then they should be suctioned.

There are mounted or portable suction devices with two types of catheter tubes available: tonsil tip which are rigid tubes or French tip which are softer and more flexible tubes. Any catheter should be measured so that it does not go past the base of the tongue. The soft catheters are useful for suctioning the nasopharynx and for removing fluids. The harder tubes should be used for the oropharynx and mouth with care not to touch the back of the mouth and cause a gag reflex. The rigid tonsil tip is preferable for removing small obstructions as they do not collapse.

Nasopharyngeal airways

A nasopharyngeal airway (NPA) is an upper airway adjunct that is inserted through a nasal passage to assist in maintaining airway patency. They can be used on semiconscious patients and on patients who have a gag reflex. The insertion of an NPA can be very painful and the tip should be well-lubricated.

Appropriate size can be determined by measuring from the tip of the patient's nose to their earlobe.

Lubricate the nostril before inserting. Move the tube carefully posteriorly. If you encounter resistance, remove slowly and try the other nostril. As you insert, rotate the airway back and forth or in a spiral direction in order to ease the insertion.

Oropharyngeal airway

An oropharyngeal airway (OPA) is an upper airway adjunct that is inserted through the mouth to assist in maintaining airway patency. It can only be used on a patient who is unconscious. It can not be used on a patient with a gag reflex as it will cause vomiting.

Appropriate size can be determined by measuring from the patient's earlobe to the teeth.

To insert the OPA, open the patient's mouth and hold the OPA upside down. Slide it in to the back of the soft palate at the point where resistance is met to a gentle insertion. At this point, rotate the OPA continuing to move it posteriorly so that the base sits against the patient's teeth. Optional methods include sideways insertion or right side up insertion with the use of a tongue depressor. These options should only be practiced if they are accepted as part of your protocol.

Complete airway obstruction removal
- Heimlich maneuver (abdominal thrusts): Can be used to clear the airway of a conscious patient however, they should not be used on a pregnant woman; instead use chest compressions. If a patient is unconscious immediately begin CPR. Abdominal thrusts can cause internal damage and a patient should be advised to see a medical practitioner for follow-up.
- Manual removal: The finger sweep should only be performed on unconscious patients. Use a hooking action and be careful not to push object in further. Never perform a blind finger sweep on a child or infant.
- Suction: Of the nasopharynx or oropharynx can be used to remove small obstructions.
- Chest thrusts: As used in CPR, can be used for pregnant women and are considered effective for dislodging obstructions from an unconscious person as they can be done concurrent with CPR ministering.

<u>Opening the airway in infant patients</u>
- Assess breathing initially from a distance before introducing the cold and scary stethoscope. Watch for chest rise and fall; assess color and movement or lack of before handling the infant.
- Use caution in positioning the head to clear the airway. Head-tilt-chin-lift can actually block the windpipe if the head is hyperextended.
- "Blow-by" may be the only possible oxygen delivery technique for a conscious infant, holding the oxygen tubing close (a couple of inches) to the nose and delivering oxygen at a rate of 6 lpm.
- For suctioning and artificial airways, correct size of equipment is crucial. Use a pediatric resuscitation tape measure.
- Often mucous can block airways in an infant and suctioning the nasopharynx will clear the airway. Suctioning can be done with a bulb syringe.
- When inserting an oropharyngeal airway, it should be held in the upright position and inserted using a tongue depressor to keep the tongue out of the way. Inserting using the rotation technique can damage the soft palate.

Tidal volume

Tidal volume is the volume of air that is inhaled during a regular or normal breath, also known as a tidal breath. Tidal volume is important to the EMT-B in that it is a measure of the depth of a patient's breath. A tidal minute can be determined by measuring the tidal volume and multiplying by the number of tidal breaths in one minute. This is a complicated procedure that requires respiratory monitoring equipment and is therefore not a procedure carried out by the EMT-B. For the EMT-B, a hand on the chest to determine the amount of chest movement during respiration can give an indication of tidal volume.

Cricoid pressure

Cricoid pressure or the Sellick maneuver is a preventative measure to block the esophagus and thus prevent gastric distention and vomiting during ventilation. It is used on unconscious patients, especially if they are receiving mask or BVM ventilation and endotracheal intubation can't be performed.

The technique consists of applying a downward pressure to the ring of cricoid cartilage that lines the bottom of the larynx. This effectively blocks the esophagus and ensures ventilated air enters the lungs.

Supplemental oxygen

Supplemental oxygen or oxygen therapy should be used in any situation where the patient would benefit from it. Indicators for oxygen therapy include:
- Can't breath without assistance
- Shock
- Cardiac arrest
- Inadequate or difficulty breathing
- Blood loss
- Smoke inhalation

Supplemental oxygen is a readily available treatment that can provide comfort and prevent hypoxia. Some people with chronic lung conditions have a high concentration of CO_2 in their blood. This condition may worsen with supplemental oxygen which will cause their rate of breathing to slow. These patients should be monitored carefully and the oxygen flow rate adjusted accordingly.

Oxygen is stored in green cylinders under pressure. Each cylinder has a valve attached to it and this valve must be attached to a regulator to control the release of the gas. To ensure the correct regulator is used, check that the pinhole pattern on the cylinder matches the pinhole pattern on the regulator. This is called the pin-indexing system and is a safety system developed to prevent regulators from being used on the wrong cylinders. A regulator will also have a flowmeter attached to it to show the volume of oxygen being delivered. Always inspect the cylinder, the seal and the valves; check the cylinder markings to confirm its contents.

Steps in connecting:
1. With valve pointing away from you and others, remove seal
2. Keeping valve pointing in a safe direction, quickly turn it on and off to clear the valve of dust
3. Attached regulator with flowmeter to valve
4. Attached oxygen delivery device
5. Turn on valve and adjust flowmeter
6. Apply to patient

Oxygen delivery equipment
A **simple mask** comes in adult and pediatric sizes. It can deliver a flow rate of 6-10 liters per minute (lpm) which is about 40 to 60% oxygen. The masks should only be used on a patient who is breathing on their own. These masks are being phased out in preference to nonrebreather masks and nasal cannula.

Nasal cannula is an oxygen delivery system that has two prongs at the end of the delivery tube which fit into the patient's nostrils and blow oxygen into them. They can deliver oxygen at a rate of 1 to 6 lpm which works out to 20% to 40% oxygen. These are easy-to-use and are indicated for use when patient is not critically hypoxic or when a nonrebreather mask can't be applied.

Nonrebreather masks come in sizes for adults, children and infants. They are the preferred method for oxygen delivery. They can deliver oxygen at a rate of 10 to 15 lpm which works out to be 70 to 100% oxygen. The one way valve prevents the patient from inhaling exhaled CO_2. It also allows the patient to inhale air from both the source and the reservoir bag without inhaling room oxygen. Always keep the flow rate high enough that the bag doesn't deflate completely when the patient inhales and make sure the bag is full before putting the mask on the patient.

Bag Valve Masks
The positioning of a bag valve mask requires perfect alignment of the patient's head or you will end up filling the stomach with air. Also, the mask must fit snugly or not enough air will get in. A snug fit of the mask and adequate rate of ventilation is difficult to achieve with one rescuer. The pop off valve should be disabled if there is one because it may not provide adequate tidal volume if it pops off at too low a pressure.

The BVM provides a smaller volume of air but a higher concentration of oxygen than the pocket mask as the air used is not an exhalation. The air quality a BVM provides makes up for the lower volume. As long as the pressure in a tidal breath is enough to cause the chest to rise and fall, it is likely enough to facilitate effective respiration.

The BVM is very effective for delivering extra oxygen as it can be connected to supplemental oxygen. It can also be used with an artificial airway. The BVM can also be used when a patient is conscious.

A bag valve mask can be used for a child who is not able to breathe adequately on their own. Ensure the mask and bag are of the right size, good mask seal is maintained and adequate chest expansion occurs. If using the BVM to assist breathing, coordinate it with the child's breath to prevent gagging or vomiting. Cricoid pressure can be employed.

For an unconscious child, squeeze the bag only until the chest begins to rise then release. The pop off valve must be disabled. Oxygen can be delivered at a rate of 10-15 lpm.

Pocket masks
The pocket mask is a barrier device for artificial ventilation. It is placed over the patient's mouth and held in place with the thumb and first finger of both hands while the rest of the fingers pull the jaw gently forward to create a good seal. Breathe into the mask at a rate of 1 breath every 4 or 5 seconds (adult). Watch the chest to be sure it is rising. If you encounter any resistance while administering breath, try repositioning to open the airway.

Although a large volume of air can be delivered using the pocket mask, this is not necessarily beneficial as this can create excessive pressure in the thoracic cavity. This makes it more difficult for the heart to pump blood during CPR.

The pocket mask is a very effective method for artificial ventilation but does not provide the protection from exposure that the bag valve mask does.

Hazards of using oxygen delivery systems
If the flow rate is too low, CO_2 can build up in the mask and cause suffocation or the reservoir bag may collapse making the patient struggle to inhale. There is much concern regarding patients with chronic obstructive pulmonary disease (COPD) receiving too much; check your local protocols. Generally, it is believed that pre-hospital oxygen therapy is safe to administer with these patients as long as it is monitored carefully. Oxygen is highly combustible and care should be taken that it is not being absorbed into fabrics. For the same reason, adhesive tape should not be used for labeling oxygen outlets. As with any pressurized gas, an oxygen cylinder can explode causing serious injury.

Pulse oximeters

A pulse oximeter is a device that is used to determine the oxygenation of the blood in a non-invasive manner. It uses infrared light absorption to determine how red and how oxygen saturated the blood is over the period of a pulse using the difference in infrared absorption between venous and arterial blood to determine the amount of oxygen being used by the tissues. The meter is attached to a transparent part of the anatomy, most often a fingertip. Although it provides a good guideline, it should be kept in mind that it does not monitor CO_2 levels of the blood or ventilation in general. This should not be used when using supplemental oxygen as it will give a false positive.

FROPVD

The Flow restricted oxygen powered ventilation device (FROPVD) is an oxygen powered device that can provide ventilation without physical input from the rescuer. Essentially, it uses high pressure (up to 50 psi) to deliver oxygen through a demand valve on a mask which is held in place by the rescuer. It can deliver 100% oxygen.

The FROPVD is not common in EMS pre-hospital care as the force that is used to deliver the oxygen can prove to be very damaging if not properly monitored. It should absolutely not be used on patients with possible obstructions including COPD, patients with possible neck injuries, children and infants.

Recovery position

The recovery position consists of laying the patient on their side with the top leg and top side arm on the ground anteriorly to prevent the patient from falling onto their back. A patient who is breathing by themselves can be placed in this position. Recovery position is a good position for keeping a clear airway in a patient who is not having difficulty breathing and does not have any other injuries. The position allows drainage from the mouth and can prevent a patient from choking on their vomit.

Respiratory diseases

Asthma
Asthma is an allergic reaction or reaction to stress that causes the smooth muscle of the bronchioles to contract; referred to as a bronchiospasm. This constricts the airways and may even completely block them. Production of excessive mucous can also block the airway further. The resulting symptoms can include coughing, wheezing, hypoxia and increased respiration rate. The patient will likely be using accessory muscles to try to catch their breath, but are actually trying to expel trapped air.

Asthma can be treated with a bronchodilator inhaler (by an EMT-B). Since it is an allergic reaction, epinephrine in inhaled form may be administered by medical practitioners.

Emphysema
Emphysema is caused by **deterioration of the alveolar walls**, with loss of elasticity and possible rupture creating large air spaces. The result is reduced gas exchange and difficulty exhaling. Since the patient can't exhale completely, they have to take deeper breaths to achieve adequate respiration. Blood oxygen can be lowered as a result. The condition usually goes undetected until the damage is extensive and causes symptoms which may include: difficulty breathing during exertion, increased time to exhale, quiet breathing but not necessarily wheezing, and increased heart rate.

Chronic bronchitis
Chronic bronchitis presents itself as a history of lung infections, excessive mucous that is loosened upon coughing, wheezing or rhonchi and difficulty breathing due to inefficient gas exchange. It is caused by an increased number of mucous cells. Their secretions smother the alveoli making it difficult for the capillaries to release CO_2.

Both emphysema and chronic bronchitis are associated with smoking and may cause heart failure.

Bronchodilators
Bronchodilators are a medication prescribed for people with asthma and other chronic pulmonary disorders. They act by dilating the bronchioles allowing air movement to occur more readily. They are normally dispensed through an inhaler which sprays the medication while the patient inhales. Usually the patient takes two "puffs" from the inhaler. Results can be quite rapid. Check your regional protocol as to whether EMT-B's are allowed to administer bronchodilators.

In order to administer this medication, the EMT-B must first verify that the patient is in need of the inhaler by showing respiratory distress, and that the patient has not recently taken a dose from the inhaler. The EMT-B must have permission from the medical overseer to go ahead with the dose.

The patient should be instructed to:
- Exhale deeply
- Wrap their lips around the inhaler mouth piece
- While pressing down on the canister inhale deeply,
- Hold their breath for as long as they feel comfortable
- Exhale and breathe normally before beginning a second puff (if prescribed for two puffs at a time)

Important terms

Acidosis: Build up of acids in the body which could be from excess glucose, poisoning or even stress. Acidosis can cause rapid breathing as the patient tries to remove excess CO_2.

Airway adjunct: A device used to assist in opening the airway by bypassing the tongue and maintaining the airway. Oropharyngeal airway adjuncts are inserted through the mouth; nasopharyngeal airway adjuncts are inserted through a nasal passage. Airway adjuncts are also referred to as artificial airways.

Apnea (Apnoea): No breathing or periods of no breathing

Auscultation: The use of a stethoscope to listen to the sound of organs in the body cavity.

Bradypnea: Slow regular breathing

BVM device: Bag valve mask device is a device for assisted breathing. The mask covers the patient's nose and mouth; the valve is one way and the bag is squeezed to deliver oxygen (breaths). The bag can also be attached to an oxygen delivery system.

Central neurogenic hyperventilation: Rapid and deep respirations characteristic of stroke victims. Can also be observed where a severe head injury is involved.

Cheyne-Stokes respirations: A pattern of breathing often seen in stroke or comatose patients; periods of apnea are interspersed with periods of tachypnea, or rapid breathing.

Dyspnea: Difficulty breathing

Hyperpnea: Fast deep breathing

Hypopnea: Slow deep breathing

Ischemia: Lack of oxygen

Patent: Open airway that is clear of obstructions

Tachypnea: Fast breathing

Cardiology

Anatomy and function

The **circulatory system** consists of the heart, the arterial system and the venous system. The *heart* acts as a pump that pushes blood to the lungs and then out through the arteries, to arterioles and then capillaries where oxygenated blood is picked up by the cells. The *arteries* are under pressure and have smooth muscle in their lining to help move blood along to the capillaries.

The *capillaries* are the midpoint between the arteries and veins at both the lungs and the cellular level. Their thin walls allow for gas exchange, and the delivery of nutrients and the removal of waste products. The *veins* and venous system is low pressure and has relatively thin walls without musculature. The venous system consists of veins, venules and capillaries. The capillaries deliver deoxygenated blood to the venules where it is moved along to the veins. This system carries blood back towards the heart for re-oxygenation and removal of CO_2.

The heart is made of cardiac muscle which is heart specific and contracts because of stimulation by the electrical impulses provided by the conduction system of the heart. The heart muscle is supplied blood by the coronary arteries which are the first branch off the aorta. The chambers of the heart are *two atriums and two ventricles*. The atria receive blood, the ventricles send blood. The right atrium receives deoxygenated blood from the Vena Cava, which is the final vein of the circulatory system. Blood moves through the tricuspid atrioventricular valve into the right ventricle. The right ventricle pumps blood into the lungs through the pulmonic valve via the pulmonary artery. Oxygenated blood returns to the heart through the left atrium, flows down through the mitral valve to the left ventricle and is pumped out through the aorta through to the rest of the body via the arteries.

Major veins and arteries directly associated with the heart:
- Aorta: Also known as the aortic arch or ascending aorta receives blood from the left ventricle and distributes it through the arterial system to the body; very thick-walled for high pressure.
- Pulmonary arteries: Receive blood from the pulmonary trunk and send it out to the lungs.
- Pulmonary veins: Return oxygenated blood from the lungs to the left atrium.
- Pulmonary trunk: Receives deoxygenated blood from the right ventricle and sends it via the pulmonary arteries to the lungs.
- Superior vena cava: Returns blood from the upper body to the heart.
- Inferior vena cava: Returns blood from the lower body to the heart.
- Left coronary artery: Supplies blood to both ventricles and the left atrium.
- Right coronary artery: Supplies blood to the right atrium.
- Coronary sinus: Received most of the deoxygenated blood from the heart muscle, receives blood from the great cardiac vein and the middle cardiac vein.

Conduction system of the heart
A small percentage of cardiac muscle cells are auto rhythmic in that they contract continually, setting the beat for the rest of the heart muscle.

The initiation of each heart beat begins in the muscle cells of the Sinoatrial (SA) Node, at the top of the right atrium. The electrical charge produced by their contraction then moves to the atrioventricular (AV) node, which lies on the wall between the right atrium and the right ventricle. The signal produced in the AV node is sent down the atrioventricular bundle, also known as the bundle of his, which lies in the wall between the right and left ventricles. From there it moves into the two branches of this bundle, known as the right and left bundle branches. At the end of the branches are the purkinje fibers, which initiate the contraction of the ventricles from the bottom up.

The result is the recognizable double beat of the heart with the contraction of the atria staggered slightly, but perfectly from that of the ventricles.

Heart attacks

A heart attack happens when the blood supply to the heart muscle is blocked. This usually occurs at the left ventricle and results in damage to the cardiac muscle at that point. The left ventricle pumps the blood to the rest of the body, and it receives oxygenated blood from the lungs via the right atrium. When its musculature isn't working, blood pools in the left ventricle. This is called **congestive heart failure** (CHF) and can result in death. Because of the compromised circulation that results, shortness of breath and increased heart rate are symptoms. Also chest noises will be heard as blood and fluid accumulate in the lungs.

A heart attack, also referred to as a myocardial infarction (MI) or acute myocardial infarction (AMI), is the result of the heart muscle not receiving blood due to a blockage of the coronary arteries. As soon as blood supply to the heart muscle or myocardial tissue stops, the tissue begins to die and this impairs the heart's ability to pump blood.

Symptoms of a heart attack include:
- Although not always painful, there may be a tightening sensation or pain within the chest which can radiate out to the left arm, neck and jaw.
- Patient can feel faint, nauseous and/or short of breath.
- They may appear pale and have damp skin.
- Their pulse may be rapid, slow or irregular.
- There will be a change in blood pressure.

The most severe consequence of heart attack is sudden death which is usually the result of congestive heart failure (CHF).

Cardiogenic shock is another consequence of a heart attack. Shock is the physiological state of a body without enough blood supply. Tissue damage caused by the initial heart attack is spread due to the inefficiency of the muscle near the damaged area. The resulting symptoms are similar to that of congestive heart failure as the heart is unable to distribute the blood it receives, which then builds up and backs up into the lungs.

Arrhythmias are irregular heart rhythms that result from the heart attack whether as a result of muscle tissue damage or malfunction of the sinoatrial node. They are often the precursor to complete heart failure (death). They are the cause of cardiac arrest.

Cardiac arrest

Cardiac arrest occurs when the heart seizes to generate an effective beat to provide circulation. This is usually a result of arrhythmias, where the heart's electrical impulse system no longer functions and a pulse is not produced. A patient can be conscious during a heart attack but once cardiac arrest occurs, they will no longer be conscious.

The muscle damage caused by a heart attack can lead to cardiac arrest. Cardiac arrest lasting 4-6 minutes leads to death due to brain damage caused by lack of oxygen to the brain.

Cardiac compromise

Cardiac compromise is a catch-all phrase to indicate that there are signs that could be associated with a heart condition. A patient who can be suspected of cardiac compromise may present the following:
- Be pale or grey in color,
- Have cold hands and feet due to poor circulation
- Be perspiring excessively
- Have a rapid or irregular pulse
- Have a feeling of impending doom or feel very anxious

CPR

The hand position for adults and children is on the lower half of the sternum at the line of the nipples. For adults, two hands and for children one or both hands can be used to compress the chest. For a child, the compression should be one-third to one-half the total depth of the chest; for an adult 1 ½ to 2 inches of compression will suffice.

When performing CPR on an infant (under 1 year), chest compressions should be done with two fingers placed on the sternum just below the nipple line. The rescuer who is performing compressions can use the 2 thumbs technique with encircling hands holding the infant.

Chest compressions during CPR provide an artificial pulse by compressing the volume of the chest and thus pushing the blood from the heart. The chest compressions to breaths ratio is 30:2 for adults, children and infants. If two rescuers are performing CPR on an infant, then the compression-to-breath ratio can be 15:2. A neonate or newborn requires 90 compressions to 60 breaths per minute.

The main idea is to get the compression of the chest happening rhythmically and effectively so that about 100 compressions per minute are achieved. The chest should completely decompress between each compression.

AEDs

It has been proven that the early use of an AED can save lives by shocking a heart that is in fibrillation into regular rhythm. The earlier it is used on a patient needing it the better.

An AED should be used on a patient who is not conscious, not breathing and shows no signs of circulation. Depending on your locality and state protocols, an AED can be used on any patient with the above symptoms who is over 8 years old and weighs more than 55 pounds. Pediatric pads may be used on a child under 8 years of age or weighing less than 55 pounds if your local EMS protocol allows for it. If the patient has a pacemaker or similar implanted device, move the pads at least 1 inch away from the device so that the electric current can flow freely between the pads.

The most common error when using an AED is that it has a low battery. Thus it is very important to check the battery on your equipment on a regular basis. Other errors are both operational and mechanical including: trying to place pads on a moving patient or trying to apply AED to a patient who is conscious and experiencing ventricular tachycardia (V-tach).

Using an AED is easier and more effective than CPR:
1. Turn on AED; battery should be in working order if proper maintenance procedures are being followed.
2. Attach electrode pads to patient's chest at landmarked points, making sure all medicated patches and any nitroglycerin paste have been removed from patient's skin. Patient and area around them should be dry. Chest area may need to be shaved for good contact.
3. Follow the voice prompts and screen instructions. Vocalize your part if the machine has a recording device. When AED states that no shock is advised, check for pulse. If there is a pulse then follow post resuscitation procedures; if no pulse, begin CPR and wait for ALS.

CPR is performed until the AED is on the scene and attached to the patient ready for use. CPR is stopped while the AED is in operation as per the voice prompts. Stopping CPR is indicated because AED is much more effective to restart a heart in fibrillation. It is important that personnel are trained effectively in the use of the AED so, that there is not more than a few seconds between stopping CPR and starting AED. Stopping CPR is necessary for the AED to determine the rhythm of the fibrillations in order to deliver the shock at the correct time.

Pulse checks are not carried out during AED as the patient should not be touched during the AED cycles. The AED shocks are delivered in stacks of three, once the three shocks have been delivered, CPR can be resumed if no pulse is detected. Continue CPR for 60 seconds and then if no pulse, repeat the AED cycles.

Post resuscitative care

The priority in post-resuscitative care becomes airway management just as any emergency call requires. This may include clearing vomitus from the airway with suction, providing ventilation and/or oxygen therapy and continuous monitoring of the patient's vital signs. If cardiac arrest re-occurs, repeat the CPR and AED procedures from the beginning. It is a good idea to keep the AED attached to the patient until they arrive at the hospital, enabling immediate use if required. The patient should be stabilized while awaiting transport.

PQRST

PQRST is a standard acronym used in EMS with the letters standing for:
- Provokes: What causes or caused the pain? With a cardiac patient this may include exertion or stress.
- Quality: What kind of pain is it? (i.e. sharp, dull or throbbing pain). For a cardiac patient, this may be described as tightness, squeezing or a heartburn type pain.
- Radiates: Does the pain move? Cardiac patients often feel the first pain in their chest and then it moves outward to the arm (left first) and neck.
- Severity: How bad does it hurt? Different people have different pain tolerance, so this can be very subjective.
- Time: When did the pain start? How long did it last or has it lasted? Angina attacks tend to last less than 20 minutes; a heart attack can last much longer.

SAMPLE history

- S--Signs and symptoms: The reason that EMS was called to the scene, EMT-B can see some obvious signs, patient and bystanders can communicate symptoms.
- A--Allergies: Ask about what allergies are known, foods and medications recently consumed, any environmental exposures and of course, look for a med-alert tag.
- M--Medications: What medications is the patient currently on? This includes prescriptions, over the counter and any recreational drugs such as marijuana or alcohol and birth control. Again, look for a medical alert tag.
- P--Pertinent past history: Any medical history relating to the current incident, previous heart problems, for instance.
- L--Last oral intake: When and how much did the patient last consume anything? This is important if a general anesthetic is necessary later.
- E--Events: Leading to the illness or injury: What did you do before this happened? If chest pain occurs when a patient is active it is more likely angina; chest pain while at rest may indicate heart attack.

Chain of survival

The chain of survival is the four step system that should be followed in a cardiac arrest scenario in a pre-hospital setting. It has been proven that following these steps in the order designated can increase a patient's chances of survival. Chain of survival is based on a heart attack situation but can be applied to any unresponsive person.

1. Early access: As soon as a person recognizes the emergency, they must contact 9-1-1.
2. Early CPR: The sooner circulation is restored the better chances of survival, even if it is through CPR.
3. Early defibrillation: As soon as an AED is available, it should be used by trained personnel.
4. Early advanced care: This can include endotracheal intubation in order to make the patient more responsive to the AED and administering medications to ensure the heart retains a regular rhythm once resuscitated.

Nitroglycerin

Nitroglycerin increases blood flow to the heart muscle by relaxing the walls of the blood vessels. For this reason, it is called a vasodilator. Its effects are nearly instantaneous. It is applied sublingually (beneath the tongue) in either a spray or tablet form.

In many states, an EMT-B is allowed to administer or help administer prescribed nitroglycerin to a patient suffering chest pains that may be due to angina. Be sure that the medication is prescribed in that patient's name and that you have the go ahead from the medical advisor before administering the medication. Nitroglycerin should be administered a maximum of three times pre-hospital. It is extremely important to monitor blood pressure when this medication is used as it is a very effective vasodilator and the drop in blood pressure that results from its use may cause hypoxia.

Hypotension

A person experiencing hypotension has low blood pressure. Low blood pressure in itself is not a sign of hypotension, other symptoms besides blood pressure lower than normal range (130/85) will be present. Low blood pressure alone is very common among very fit individuals such as athletes. A person with hypotension will feel faint or dizzy and weak. Causes of hypotension are reduced blood volume (for example by blood loss or dehydration) or inefficient circulation which can be a result of impaired heart function or medications. Some heart related causes of hypotension are cardiac muscle damage due to disease or heart attack, valve malfunction or a malfunction in the conductive system of the heart.

Hypertension

A patient exhibiting hypertension will show a consistently high blood pressure above 140/90. A high normal, above 130/85, can also be suspect. Hypertension can be the result of lifestyle, metabolic defects or heredity. Although the actual cause is not always known, the result is that the heart is working under extreme pressure and the arteries are also under that same pressure. Hypertension, "the silent killer," can go undiagnosed for years then appear as target organ damage and this is when these patients will appear in the EMS. The target organs are usually the kidneys, the brain and the heart. Hypertension is the most common cause of cardiac arrest due to damage of the coronary arteries through atherosclerosis.

Angina

Angina and heart attack are similar in that they both are a result of decreased or eliminated blood flow to the heart muscle, which affects its ability to contract and produce an effective pulse. Angina or, more correctly, angina pectoris, is the chest pain that results when a partial blockage of the coronary arteries leads to a poor blood supply to the heart muscle. The reduced blood supply depletes oxygen available to the muscle cells (hypoxia) and makes it hard for them to contract. Essentially, it is like a cramp in the heart muscle. An angina attack commonly occurs during times of physical stress when the heart is working hard and needs more oxygen.

A heart attack is when complete blockage occurs in a coronary artery and muscle tissue of the heart begins to die. Whereas an angina attack can be short and periodic, a heart attack is the same pain only continuous and lasting for up to several hours. A heart attack can be unprovoked and can occur any time. Angina pain can be alleviated with nitroglycerin.

Stable angina is often the first occurrence of angina as a symptom of coronary artery disease (CAD) and the resulting ischemia. It presents itself as chest pain that occurs when the heart is exerted i.e. going upstairs. As the condition worsens, it becomes unstable angina and can occur more frequently and with less exertion. It is usually the result of the plaque that has built up in the artery actually damaging the wall of the artery. This causes the body to try to heal it with blood clotting platelets. The "scab" that is formed increases the blockage even more, subsequently increasing the ischemia of the effected tissue.

Variant angina or Prinzmetal's syndrome is a type of unstable angina where the diseased artery goes into spasm. Unstable angina is always a cardiac emergency.

ACLS

CLS (ALS) is advanced cardiac life support, which are clinical interventions beyond the EMT-B's scope of practice. They include insertion of intravenous (IV) drip and monitoring the patient with electrocardiogram equipment. The EMT-B, upon being called to a possible cardiac compromise situation, should immediately arrange for ACLS to come to the scene.

Pulse

When the left ventricle pumps blood into the arteries, their elasticity causes them to expand as they receive the oxygenated blood. This expansion is called a pulse. The pulse should be rhythmic and have a rate of between 70 to 80 beats per minute (bpm). Medications such as beta blockers can have an effect on this rate, and people with hypertension will have a higher pulse. People who are very fit tend to have a lower resting pulse; as low as 60 bpm is not unusual. Hypotensive patients may also show a reduced pulse.

The pulse can be felt upon palpitation of an artery that lies over a bone. The pulse is strongest and easiest to detect in arteries closest to the heart. Common pulse check points are:

- At the wrist on the radial artery
- At the medial (inside) of the biceps on the brachial artery
- At the neck just outside of the larynx on the common carotid artery

When taking the pulse, use the index and middle finger pressed over the artery, not so hard as to restrict blood flow. Never take a pulse with your thumb as your own pulse will interfere. Pulse can be approximated by counting for 15 seconds and multiplying by four.

Blood pressure

Blood pressure is usually taken with a cuff and pressure gauge called a **sphygmomanometer**. The cuff is wrapped around the upper arm to take the pressure reading from the brachial artery. The bulb on the gauge is used to pump pressure into the cuff until the artery is occluded. Then the pressure is slowly released as a stethoscope is held over the brachial artery to listen. The first sound heard is the result of ventricular contraction and the pressure reading on the gauge at that time is called the **systolic blood pressure**. As the pressure is released further, it reaches a point where it is equal to the pressure in the arteries when the ventricles are relaxed. The reading on the gauge is the **diastolic blood pressure**.

ASA administration

Many states are allowing their EMT-B personnel to administer acetylsalicylic acid (ASA) to patients experiencing chest pain that might indicate cardiac compromise. It has been shown that the anticoagulating properties of ASA can markedly reduce the severity of a heart attack. The administration of any medication is always under direct supervision from the medical overseer. Proper documentation is essential.

ASA can be administered to patients experiencing chest pain that is indicative of a heart attack or angina if they do not respond to their prescribed nitroglycerin or the chest pain lasts for more than 15 minutes.

ASA should not be administered to patients who may be bleeding internally, allergic to ASA or who have recently taken ASA (within the last 24 hours). Nor should it be given to patients who have recently used sildenafil citrate (Viagra) or other vasodilating prescriptions. The vasodilation combined with the "blood thinning" properties of ASA could cause a severe drop in blood pressure.

Important terms

Acute myocardial infarction (AMI): A heart attack is occurring or more succinctly death of cardiac muscle is occurring.

Angina: Squeezing or crushing like chest pain that last a few minutes at a time; associated with the heart muscle not receiving enough blood to contract easily.

Aneurysm: The bulging out of an arterial wall at a weak point. Weaknesses in the walls are often created by atherosclerosis. These weak points can burst and cause a person to bleed to death.

Asymptomatic: Condition that presents no symptoms that are apparent to the patient.

Atherosclerosis: A form of arteriosclerosis where the walls of arteries thicken due to an increase in smooth muscle fiber and fatty deposits known as plaque. This condition is often associated with coronary artery disease.

Arrhythmias: Irregular heart rhythms that are often associated with heart attacks resulting in death.

Arteriosclerosis: A disease which results in the hardening of arteries due to thickening and loss of elasticity. Note: It is a common mistake to refer to arteriosclerosis as the calcification of artery walls and atherosclerosis as fatty plaque thickening of artery walls

Bradycardia: Heart rhythm is slow, less than 60 bpm

Cardiac output: The volume of blood pumped through the heart in one minute, affected by blood pressure and heart rate.

Coronary artery disease (CAD): Disease of the coronary arteries that causes them to narrow and reduces blood flow to the cardiac muscle. CAD can be caused by atherosclerosis, spasms of the coronary artery or blood clots.

Diasystole: The relaxation phase of the heart beat, when the ventricles open up to receive blood from the atria.

Embolus: Any debris floating through the bloodstream; it could be a blood clot, or other debris caused by an injury that breaks lose and enters the bloodstream. An embolus can block an artery and prevent blood flow to a major organ such as the heart thus becoming an "obstruction."

Hypoperfusion syndrome (shock): Oxygen and nutrients are not reaching the tissues of the body as a result of poor circulation or lack of blood volume.

Perfusion: Sufficient blood flow to cells or tissues.

Symptomatic: Condition that presents with symptoms that are noted by the patient

Systole: Contraction phase of the heart beat, specifically the ventricles as they eject blood outward to the aorta and the lungs.

Tachycardia: Heart rhythm that is more than 100 bpm

Thrombus: Term used to describe a blood clot that has broken loose from the blood vessel wall.

Ventricular fibrillation: Heart muscles twitch and vibrate but do not produce an actual beat or contraction therefore no circulation of blood occurs.

Ventricular tachycardia: Heart rate is fast over an extended period, too fast to create enough pressure to produce a pulse, thus not achieving adequate circulation. Electrical impulses originate from the ventricle.

Trauma

Circulatory system

Veins are vessels that carry blood back to the heart. The major veins in the circulatory system are:
- Femoral vein: Each leg, inner thigh
- Jugular veins: Neck on either side of the trachea, from the brain and head.
- Pulmonary veins: From the lungs to the heart
- Renal veins: From the kidneys
- Superior vena cava: Upper body to the heart
- Inferior vena cava: Lower body to the heart

Arteries are vessels that carry blood away from the heart. The major arteries are:
- Abdominal aorta: From the aortic arch through the abdomen
- Renal artery: To the kidneys
- Carotid arteries: Neck on either side of the trachea, feeds the brain and head
- Pulmonary arteries: From heart to lungs
- Coronary arteries: Blood supply for the cardiac muscle
- Femoral artery: Each leg, inner thigh
- Brachial artery: Each arm, inside

Baseline vital signs

Baseline vital signs are taken during the focused physical exam after initial assessment. They include:
- Level of consciousness: If the patient is unconscious use the Glasgow coma score. With a conscious patient, ask questions. Are they restless or irritable?
- Pulse: Taken at the wrist. Time for 15 seconds and multiply out to get the full minute.
- Respirations: Determine the breaths per one minute and assess the quality of the breathing.
- Skin: To assist in determining the quality of circulation. Feel for temperature and dampness. Observe skin color.
- Capillary refill: The nail blanch test helps determine quality of circulation. Press nail bed with your finger and count the seconds it takes to go from white to pink. A pulse oximeter can also be used to determine quality of circulation.

Glasgow coma scale

The Glasgow coma scale (GCS) is a standardized scale used to assess brain injury or level of consciousness. Scoring evaluates three response parameters:
- Eye response: 1-no eye opening, 2-open to pain, 3-open to voice, 4- open spontaneously.
- Verbal response: 1-no response, 2-makes incomprehensible sounds, 3-uses inappropriate words, 4-shows confusion, 5-orientated, able to communicate.
- Motor response: 1- no response, 2- extends to painful stimulus, 3 – flexion to painful stimulus, 4 – pulls away from painful stimulus, 5 – patient can indicate where pain is, 6 – patient can follow commands.

Each parameter is evaluated on a decreasing scale, with 3 being the lowest possible score. Any score lower than 8 is considered a severe brain injury. The (GCS) is part of the trauma score.

DCAP-BTLS

DCAP-BTLS is a mnemonic used to remember the detailed physical exam carried out on trauma patients if, after initial assessment, the patient has not been transported immediately. The letters stand for:

- **D**eformity
- **C**ontusions
- **A**brasions
- **P**unctures
- **B**urns
- **T**enderness
- **L**acerations
- **S**welling

The DCAP-BTLS sequence is a thorough inspection where each part of the body is inspected for the above symptoms. The inspection moves systematically, starting at the head and neck, the chest, the abdomen, the pelvis, the extremities and then the posterior side of the body. Securing the neck, listening for breathing, abdominal sounds, and palpations are incorporated into the inspection and once completed baseline vital signs are taken.

Revised trauma score

The revised trauma score is a triage technique used by emergency personnel to determine the severity of the patient's trauma. It helps to determine if a patient needs to be transported and to which treatment cent. The score is based on values applied to the Glasgow coma scale (GCS), the systolic blood pressure and the respiratory rate.

GCS
- 13 to15 point on the GCS scores 4
- 9 to 12 scores 3
- 6 to 8 scores 2
- Less than 4 scores 0

Systolic numbers are assigned as follows:
- Above 89mmHg is given the score of 4
- Between 88 and 76 mmHg scores 3, from 50 to 75 mmHg is scored 2
- Between 1 and 49 mmHg is given a score of 1
- No blood pressure receives the score 0

Respiratory rate
- 10 to 29 breaths per minute is scored as 4
- Higher than 29 is considered a 3
- 6 to 9 breaths per minute is given a 2
- 1 to 5 gets scored 1
- 0 is given to non breathers

Rapid trauma assessment

After the scene survey and initial assessment, the rapid trauma assessment is used if it appears that the mechanism of injury (MOI) warrants it; for instance, a pedestrian-car incident. It is important to reconsider the MOI once you have done the initial assessment as there may be things you missed when you first arrived on the scene. Once airway has been established and bleeding has been controlled, carry out the rapid trauma assessment, also referred to as the DCAP-BTLS sequence. Important factors to remember are:
- Apply appropriate size cervical collar immediately after inspection of head and neck.
- Painful areas do not always need to be palpated! Do not palpate a painful pelvis.
- Decision to transport can be made at any point during the Rapid Trauma Assessment.

Car accident injury

The law of conservation of energy states that energy can't be created or destroyed. Anything in motion is considered to have energy and can be described as a force.

Newton's first law is "A body in motion remains in motion until a force is applied to change it." In a motor vehicle accident (MVA), the motion is the movement of the vehicle and the force applied to the vehicle is either: another vehicle, a solid object or road conditions that cause the vehicle to lose control.

A vehicle moving at 50 mph that hits a tree will come to a sudden stop. The force (energy) required to stop the vehicle is essentially applied by the tree and absorbed by the vehicle and the passengers. In addition, the passengers are still moving (remaining in motion) at 50 mph when the car hits the tree, so they are going to hit the interior of the vehicle, or the restraining system at 50 mph. Finally, organs inside the passenger's body hit the skeleton at 50 mph. This makes for three levels of impact in one MVA.

Mechanism of injury: If unrestrained, a person in a motor vehicle will hit the windshield with their head, and may even be launched from the car. Also, the impact of the steering wheel and dashboard can be expected to cause internal abdominal injuries and pelvic/leg injuries. Even when restrained by a seatbelt, ribcage fractures and abdominal injuries can be expected.

Head-on collisions will provide twice as much impact. In rollovers, the victims can be hit from all sides including vertical impact on top of the head. Rear end collisions commonly cause neck and torso injuries. When arriving on the scene, look at the vehicle the patient was removed from in order to have an idea of where your patient may have injuries.

Injuries can be internal or external. Those that are internal are obviously more difficult to determine and the EMT-B should consider the mechanism of injury to help guide them in the assessment of a patient. The angle and speed of contact are important in knowing what to look for.

A car accident victim will have injuries that reflect where the person's body made contact with the inside of the vehicle. If someone has fallen and landed on their back, injuries to ribs, back and internal organs should be considered. Direct force to a limb will cause a different type of damage than a twisting force.

The following types of incidents result in different types of injuries:

- No seat belt: With no seat belt there is a much greater chance of being ejected from the vehicle. Bodies ejected from the vehicle have less than 30% survival statistically. There is an increased chance of spinal injury and impact with the windshield will produce severe head injuries. Impact with other passengers is another serious implication. Often children can be severely injured by an unrestrained adult tossed about the car.
- Lap belt only: If the patient was only wearing a lap belt, there will be impact with the dashboard and the steering wheel and possibly the windshield, resulting in injury to the face, head and neck.
- Shoulder strap only: If only the shoulder is restrained, the results can be severe neck and shoulder injuries and possible decapitation.

Falls

The first law of thermodynamics, a.k.a. the law of conservation of energy, states that energy can't be created or destroyed. Newton's second law states that force is equal to mass times acceleration.

When someone falls, the distance they fall combined with the resistance of the surface they hit will have significant impact on the extent of their injuries. Bodies accelerate at the speed of gravity when they fall; about 30 feet per second. A heavier person will land with much more force than a lighter person.

A body will absorb whatever energy the surface doesn't absorb, so injuries will depend on whether they land on something solid and hard like concrete or something soft like piles of garbage bags.

Child vs. adult injuries

When an adult is hit by a car, the impact is usually below the thighs hitting the bumper. As they fold forward and hit the hood of the car, the hips and torso hit the hood and then they slide off and hit the pavement. A child's first impact is dependent on their height, the bumper could hit anywhere from shoulders and head down. A taller child will then fold over the hood of the car and hit with thorax and abdomen. Both victims can suffer head injuries from contact with the windshield or when they fall to the pavement.

When an adult falls, fractures of the wrist, hip and spine can be suspected. Children tend to fall head first because the head is the heaviest part of their body.

Stab wounds

Stab wounds are penetration wounds that can result in much more internal bleeding than is indicated by their external appearance. The severity can depend on the location, the length of the blade and the depth penetrated.

A stab wound that starts in the chest can point downward and injure abdominal organs or an upward stab from the abdomen can reach into the thoracic cavity penetrating lungs or nick major veins and arteries. A single penetration can be misleading as the stabber may have moved the knife around once the skin was penetrated, resulting in much more internal damage.

Shock

Shock is hypoperfusion, or the lack of blood supply to tissues. The type of shock defines what is causing the hypoperfusion:
- Hypovolemic shock: Due to loss of blood volume caused by bleeding or severe dehydration.
- Cardiogenic shock: The heart is not functioning sufficiently for effective circulation.
- Neurogenic shock: Caused by injury to the nervous system, including the spinal cord or brain; damage to the sympathetic nervous system.
- Anaphylactic shock: A severe allergic response where the body releases excessive histamine which causes vasodilation and a dramatic reduction in blood pressure.
- Septic shock: From infection, usually bacterial, that leads to tissue damage and affects circulation.

Typical signs of shock are:
Compensated shock: Where the body is still try to make up for blood loss
- Slight increase in heart rate, blood pressure normal or a little high
- Lethargic, irritability, slight confusion
- Skin is cool and damp
- Rapid breathing

Decompensated shock
- Moderate increase in heart rate, weak pulse, blood pressure below normal
- Confused or unconscious, dilated pupils
- Skin begins to turn grey or bluish, especially at lips and nail beds as oxygenated blood is reduced
- Rapid and shallow breathing

Advanced shock
- Coma
- Heart rate less than 60 bpm, blood pressure extremely low.
- Excessive perspiration
- Slow and ineffective breathing

Emergency care of a shock victim: As always, airway management is priority when treating any patient. Open airway, if necessary, provide oxygen, use a BVM to assist in ventilations if patient is having difficulty breathing or, use more advanced measures as necessary.

Next, control any obvious bleeding. Once this is done, place patient in a supine position with feet elevated and keep them warm with blankets. Transport the patient immediately.

Bleeding

Recognizing the origin of bleeding can help in determining the severity of a patient's injury.

- Arterial bleeding implies the injury is quite deep as arteries tend to be more internal. Blood will spurt with pulses as it is pumped from the heart. It is freshly oxygenated so it will be bright red. Because it comes out at such high pressure and volume, this is the most difficult bleeding to control and blood loss can result in reduced blood pressure very quickly.
- Venous bleeding has a steady flow and the blood is dark and deoxygenated. The injury will not be as deep as veins tend to be closer to the surface of the body. This bleeding is much easier to control due to a lower volume, easier access and less or no pressure behind the flow.
- Capillary bleeding tends to be minimal, with dark red deoxygenated blood. This is usually from surface cuts and scrapes that can be controlled easily.
- Internal bleeding has the biggest risk because bleeding can go undetected until blood loss is serious and the patient shows signs of hypovolemic shock.

Signs of internal bleeding are:
- Bleeding from mouth, nose, vagina, rectum
- Swelling and tenderness in area of bleeding
- Black or bright red blood in stool or vomit
- Abdominal bleeding can present as a distended abdomen
- Signs of shock, such as excessive thirst, rapid breathing and reduced blood pressure

The emergency care is limited to treating for shock and elevating the area, if possible, above the heart.

Tourniquet use: A tourniquet is only recommended in extreme circumstances where arterial bleeding needs to be controlled. Severe tissue damage may be caused by a tourniquet. The tourniquet should be a bandage a minimum of four inches wide applied to the proximal side of the wound as close as possible to the wound to minimize tissue damage. Important points to remember are:
- The time the tourniquet was applied should be documented and communicated to all personnel dealing with the patient.
- Never apply a tourniquet over a joint.
- The tourniquet should never be covered; this may cause it to be overlooked.
- Never loosen a tourniquet once it has been applied. This could cause a severe drop in blood pressure.

External bleeding: The very first thing that must be done is to establish and secure the airway. Then the EMT-B can address the bleeding, if it is severe enough to be a priority. Generally, using a sterile dressing and applying direct pressure is the recommended technique to control bleeding. Pressure causes blood flow to slow down and thus enables clotting. To further reduce blood flow, elevate the wound (if possible) above the heart and head. Sometimes additional pressure points need to be considered, applying pressure to a supplying artery can help reduce blood flow to the area.

Other approaches may include setting fractured bones using a splint or pressure splint. Once a pressure bandage has been applied, it shouldn't be removed as this may destroy any clotting that has started to occur. Instead, apply more dressing.

Burns

The skin is the largest organ of the body. It protects the internal tissues and organs from physical damage, infection and dehydration. It provides temperature regulation through the evaporation of sweat and the regulation of blood flow to the skin's surface. It is also responsible for the production of vitamin D. The sense of touch is provided by the hairs and nerves of the skin.

Skin is made up of two layers: the epidermis and the dermis. The epidermis consists of a thin layer of tough flat cells. The dermis is a much thicker connective tissue layer which contains nerves, capillaries, sweat glands and hair follicles, with a fatty layer at its base.

Classification of burns:
- First degree burns or superficial burns are burns that have only penetrated the epidermis. They tend to be red, very painful and may be moist.
- Second degree burns or partial thickness burns are burns that have penetrated to the second layer of skin, the dermis. They tend to be very sore, red and swollen and they will produce blisters.
- Third degree burns or full thickness burns are burns that have penetrated the full layer of dermis or deeper. They are not painful because the nerves have been destroyed. They can be white, black or red and dry.

The depth of the burn and the percentage of skin surface that it covers are the primary determinants of the severity of a burn. Factors that constitute critical burn situations are:
- Location of the burn
  - Burns to the face and mouth can mean burns or damage to the airway.
  - Third degree burns to hands, feet or genitalia are considered severe
  - Burns that cover an entire limb or body part
- Age of patient
  - The surface of skin on a small child is a larger percentage of the body
  - Seniors may have less effective immune systems and thinner skin
- Electrical burns: There is usually internal burning that can't be determined.
- Degree of burn combined with percentage of body burned
  - 10% 3rd degree burn
  - 30% 2nd degree burn

Causes of burns and treatment:
- Thermal: Burns caused by fire, steam, and hot liquids: remove any part that is still burning for example smoldering clothing or hot jewelry.
- Electrical: From lightning or electricity: Ensure patient and area are non-conducting before entering scene or touching patient. Most electrical burns are internal.
- Chemical: Acid spills, reactive reagents: Ensure you are fully protected with proper clothing and safety glasses, dust off any powders before flushing with water.
- Other causes of burns are sunlight and radiation.

Rule of nines: The rule of nines is a standard method used to quickly estimate the percentage of the body that has been burned. It divides the body into nine percent portions, or multiples of nine, based on the hand being equivalent to 1%. This rule does not apply to children as their proportions aren't the same as an adult.

The rules are:
- Head and neck: 9%
- Each Arm: 9%
- Torso front: 18%
- Torso back: 18%
- Each leg: 18%
- Perineum: 1%

Treatment: Once personal safety has been addressed and you are able to approach the patient, remove anything that is still burning: clothing or hot jewelry or chemical that is still on the body.

Next ensure the airway is clear. Then, cool the burn area as fast as possible. This is preferably done with sterile saline or sterile water, but if cool tap water is all that is available use it. With a chemical burn, continuous flushing with the water is a good idea to wash away any remaining chemical and neutralize any further reaction.

Infection is a major concern with burns. Once the area has been cooled with water, cover lightly with sterile dressing. Never apply ointments, try to break blisters or remove damaged skin. Keep patient warm and remove any wet clothing. Hypothermia can be a concern when patients are wet and cold and waiting for transport.

Nervous system

The nervous system is made up of the following components: **The Central Nervous System** (CNS) which consists of the brain and the spinal cord. The CNS is protected by bone and contains cerebrospinal fluid within it and the **Peripheral Nervous System** (PNS), which is the communication link between the rest of the body and the CNS. This can be divided further into:
- Motor: Nerves that send signals from the CNS to the muscles and glands.
- Sensory: Nerves that send signals from the body back to the brain.

The PNS can also be designated into:
- Somatic: Voluntary movement, such as walking and eating
- Autonomic: Involuntary responses, such as hunger and breathing. The sympathetic and parasympathetic nervous systems are part of the autonomic nervous system.

The cells of the nervous system are long, specialized cells called ganglia or neurons
The CNS has two protective layers: the meninges and the bones of the skull and vertebral column. The meninges are a triple layer of protective membrane that surrounds the brain and the spinal cord. The thick outer layer or meninx is called the dura mater, the middle layer is called the arachnoid layer, due to its spider web like appearance and the pia mater is the innermost layer.

The vertebral or spinal column can be divided into 5 sections from the top down:
1. Cervical: Of the neck, having 7 vertebrae (vertebrae 1-5 contain nerves for heart and lung function)
2. Thoracic: Of the chest, having 12 vertebrae
3. Lumbar: Of the abdominal area, having 5 vertebrae
4. Sacral: The pelvic region, having 5 vertebrae
5. Coccygeal: The tailbone, fused in adults over ~30, 4 vertebrae.

34

The flight or fight response is a reaction of the sympathetic nervous system to fearful or stressful stimuli. The release of adrenaline results in the increase of heart rate and respirations, dilation of pupils and constriction of blood vessels. The blood vessels constrict at the kidneys, digestive system and on the skin's surface. Sweat glands open up. The results of this response can include dry mouth, pale clammy skin, possible release of bowel and bladder. Endorphins are also released which are the body's natural painkillers.

Spinal cord damage or brain injury

Signs of spinal cord damage or brain injury include:
- Paresthesia of one or more extremity
- Loss of bladder or bowel control
- Priapism (a painful penile erection)
- Neurogenic shock
- Breathing difficulties
- Pupils dilated, different sized or non-responsive to light
- Change in mental status
- Leakage of cerebrospinal fluid from injury ears or nose

Spine board considerations
When using a spine board for a suspected spinal injury, the patient should first be stabilized with a cervical collar. Then three people (preferably) should be involved in placing the patient on the board. One person stabilizes the head and neck at all times and is responsible for calling the shots. The patient is rolled forward, the board is placed beneath him and then he is lowered onto the board. During the roll forward, an assessment of the posterior side should be carried out.

Note that the cervical collar is not sufficient to hold the neck stable especially during transport. Extra padding should be placed around the head, neck and shoulders to provide additional support to the neck. This is especially the case with pediatric patients and those wearing a helmet. Also, use extra padding if the spine injury or other injuries do not allow for the patient to be placed in the normal supine position.

Cervical collar use
If a spinal injury is suspected for any reason, manual stabilization of the spine should be performed immediately. Once the assessment of the head and neck are complete then the cervical collar can be applied. While maintaining alignment, measure the neck from the top of the shoulder to the bottom of the jaw using your hand as a measuring guide then adjust the collar size. Proper fitting is crucial - a poorly fit collar can make the injury worse or even cause more injury.

To apply the collar, fit the chin first and then wrap the rest around maintaining neutral stabilization the entire time. The cervical collar is not enough to immobilize the neck and manual support should be continued until the patient is on a spine board and padding has been placed around the head and neck.

Whiplash
Whiplash is hyperextension of the neck most often the result of rear end collisions. The injury is named for the whip-like movement of the head and neck during a sudden stop. The result is essentially a sprained neck; this can include torn or overstretched ligaments and tendons and lots of inflammation especially of the intervertebral discs. The symptoms can include numbness and tingling down the arms and into the fingers, pain in the neck, back and jaw, and headache. Whiplash associated disorder can last up to a year or more.

Other injuries

Amputated body parts: Treating the patient always takes priority over trying to save parts of the body that are no longer attached. However, if bleeding has been controlled and the body part is found, even the smallest piece is worth trying to save. The piece should be cleaned of any excess dirt that is stuck to it if doing so will not damage the tissue further. Keep the piece dry. Wrap it in bandage, gauze or anything else that is available that is dry and clean. If possible, it is helpful to keep the piece as cool as possible, but not at the risk of it getting wet. Put it in a sealed plastic bag before placing it on ice. Do not let the piece come in contact with water.

Chest trauma: It is important to consider the mechanism of injury to decide if a chest wound should be suspected. A closed chest wound can be difficult to identify and can often be overlooked if it is in combination of other injuries. Difficulty breathing and chest pain, along with pain upon palpitation can be indicative of a chest wound. The patient may exhibit signs of shock, rapid heart beat (tachycardia) and low blood pressure. Upon auscultation, a bubbling sound in the chest or the heart beat sounding distant are also indications. An open chest wound is more obvious, as is a wound in the chest area with bubbly blood or coughing up bubbly blood. Note: All chest injury patients should be given supplemental oxygen.

Pericardial tamponade: Increased fluid or bleeding into the pericardial cavity, the pressure that results reduces the volume of blood that can be pumped. Patient will be short of breath, may have enlarged neck veins and might have a weakened distal pulse. The most an EMT-B can do is administer oxygen, ensure the patient is comfortable and monitor for signs of shock. Transport as soon as possible. Treatment may require puncturing and draining of the pericardium, but this is obviously beyond the EMT-B scope of practice.

Sucking chest wound: An open wound of the chest where, because of the natural mechanics of breathing, negative pressure pulls air into the thoracic cavity upon inhalation. As these tend to be puncture wounds, they are also essentially a one way valve and air builds up in the thoracic cavity creating a pneumothorax. Symptoms will include a bubbling or sucking sound coming from the wound and shortness of breath. Treatment is oxygen. Transport as soon as possible.

Flail chest: Flail chest can be identified by watching the patient's chest move as they breathe. The segmented portion of the ribs will not move with the rest of the ribcage. This can be felt upon palpitation. It is extremely painful. The biggest concern with flail chest is that at the very least, there will be bruising to the organs underneath or worse hemorrhage. Provide oxygen and assisted breathing with a BVM if necessary. Support the fragment with a bulky loose bandage to reduce its movement. Do not apply pressure.

Hemothorax: Hemothorax or hemothorax is a build up of blood within the pleural cavity. It can cause shortness of breath and muffle the sounds of breathing but often is not detectable without x-ray. If hemothorax is suspected due to the mechanism of injury, treat with oxygen and transport immediately. Monitor for shock.

Pneumothorax: Pneumothorax may not be detected if it is confined to the pleural cavity, but if it enters the thoracic cavity and air is not being released, symptoms will be more obvious. They will show as shortness of breath and a weak pulse at the extremities. Knowing the mechanism of injury will help determine if pneumothorax is present. Treatment is supplemental oxygen and monitor for shock.Pneumothorax is also known by lay people as a "collapsed lung." The term actually refers to air (pneumo) entering the thoracic cavity. It is a result of air from the lungs or a wound leaking into the pleural or thoracic space. The air builds up as it is not exhaled and this builds pressure against the lungs, limiting their ability to expand. A small pneumothorax may heal itself.

Tension pneumothorax: This is where the pneumothorax build up enough pressure that it causes the other organs within the thoracic cavity to be dislodged. The heart is pushed up against the working lung and the trachea is also pushed in that direction. Major arteries and veins as well as the heart are subject to excess pressure. This can be fatal. Tension pneumothorax is easily identified because of the large amount of air that is trapped in the thoracic cavity. This causes breathing to be very shallow and produces a hollow sound when the chest is tapped. The trachea can appear deformed as it is pushed out of its normal position. The patient will likely be exhibiting signs of shock as the cardiopulmonary system succumbs to the pressure within the chest. Treat for shock, including assisted breathing with high oxygen and a BVM. Transport immediately.

Spontaneous pneumothorax: When air enters the pleural cavity without associated trauma to indicate an injury to the lungs. There are many causes including cancer, a ruptured cyst or a lung infection.

Impaled objects: Never remove an impaled object unless it interferes with CPR or must be removed for transport. Supplemental oxygen is always recommended. Check for exit wounds. Secure the object so that it does not move at all and transport immediately. If object needs to be shortened for transport, make sure the impaled part does not move at all while the excess is being removed. If you do have to remove the impaled object, work under direction of the EMS medical direction. If an object is impaled in the eye, both eyes should be kept covered because normally both eyes move at the same time.

Eye injury

The surface of the eyeball is the sclera or the white of the eye. It is covered with a clear protective coating called the cornea and further protected on the exposed surface by a thin membrane that lines the eyelid and the front of the eyeball called the conjunctiva. The eyeball sits safely within the eye socket of the skull and is protected further by the eyelid and eyelashes.

The eye is connected to the brain through the optic nerve. The optic nerve along with the central retinal artery and vein are encapsulated in dura mater up to the point of entry into the eyeball. The eyeball is filled with two types of fluid: irreplaceable vitreous humor in the back and aqueous humor in the front. The iris is a circular muscle that surrounds the pupil, which is the tunnel where light enters into the eyeball. The contraction of the iris cells controls the diameter of the pupil. The lens sits beneath the iris and focuses light onto the retina lining the back of the eyeball. The retina captures patterns of light with light sensitive cells and sends the picture to the brain via the optic nerve.

Most serious eye injuries require immediate transport so they can be treated by an ophthalmologist. Chemical burns or irritants in the eyes can be removed or treated by flushing generously and gently with sterile saline solution. As long as it is on the surface of the eyeball, a particle can be flushed out with copious amounts of saline. Always flush from the tear ducts outward. Remove contacts if there is a chemical burn. If there is something stuck under the eyelid you can try to remove it with a cotton swab.

Blunt force trauma can cause damage to the retina, optic nerve or the eyeball, even causing the eyeball to actually pop out. Indications can include inability to track objects with both eyes; unevenly responding pupils or a non-responding pupil. If the eye pops out, keep it covered with moist sterile dressing and try to secure it so that it does not become detached. If the eyelid is cut, keep it covered with moist, loose dressing.

Abdominal wounds

If a patient is showing signs of shock without any other symptoms there is a good chance there is an abdominal hemorrhage. Bruising in the abdominal area and lower back, painful palpitation in the area and distention are all signs of hemorrhage. Treat for shock, administer oxygen and place in the shock position, with knees and hips bent as comfortably as possible to release stomach muscle tension.

Internal abdominal bleeding is very often from the spleen or the liver due to their size and relatively external positioning. These organs, because of their blood filtering function, have an extensive blood supply and can lose blood at a rapid rate.

Tubular organs of the digestive system contain food, waste, digestive enzymes and bacteria. If they are ruptured and begin to leak into the abdominal cavity, infection is imminent. If an organ is exposed or protruding due to an open abdominal injury, do not attempt to push it back in place. Instead keep it moist with sterile saline and cover it loosely.

Limb or extremity injuries

Knowing whether the force that was applied to the bone or joint was direct, indirect or rotational will give a good idea of what type of injury was sustained. A direct force such as crushing or compression will cause fractures such as hairline, fragmenting or partial breaks of bone or joints. Indirect force applied to the extremity, such as falling onto the shoulder can cause fractures and dislocations further up, as well as compression of joint injuries like sprains and spinal compression. Twisting forces can dislocate joints closest to the force applied or cause spiral fractures that are sometimes hard to detect but still very painful.

Index of suspicion

Index of suspicion is the use of logic, combined with an understanding of the mechanism of injury and your medical training as an EMT to know where to look for injuries. If you see that the dashboard was inside a patient's abdomen prior to their removal from the accident vehicle, you can suspect abdominal injury. If a patient fell 20 feet and landed on their back, there would be a high index of suspicion that there is a spinal injury.

Bone injuries

Bone injuries are referred to as fractures and they can be open or closed. Open means that the skin is broken and closed means the trauma has not penetrated the skin. Either way, bleeding is an issue. If the injury is closed the bleeding will show as bruising and swelling. Sometimes you can see the break, but hairline fractures and spiral fractures may not be apparent and may not even show much bruising or inflammation. Often a patient can still move a fractured extremity. A more significant fracture will appear as a deformity.

The wound of the open fracture must be treated before splinting, although control of bleeding might include setting the bone and stabilizing it with a splint. An ice pack applied indirectly to the injured area will reduce pain and swelling. Even if you aren't certain there is a fracture, splint an injured extremity. Monitor for shock.

A concern with extremity fractures is that the blood supply to the rest of the limb will be interrupted. Controlling bleeding, inflammation, and splinting can help prevent this.

<u>Applying splints:</u> When a fracture or sprain is suspected, a splint should be applied but splinting should never take priority over treating other critical injuries or symptoms. The splint should be applied to the bone or joint in the position it was found in. Never attempt to reset a bone or joint unless: distal pulse is non-existent, the airway is compromised due to the injury, or transport time is longer than an hour and splinting is impossible without re-alignment. For a fracture, immobilize the joint above and below the fracture as well as the injured bone itself. For a joint injury immobilize the bone on either end of the joint. Always perform an assessment of the area distal to the injury prior to applying the splint. Take a distal and proximal pulse to get an idea of how the injury is affecting circulation and also to give a comparable for after splinting. Test for sensation and movement also. After splinting, re-check the distal pulse and response to touch to ensure you haven't compromised circulation. Assess movement to ensure you have immobilized appropriately.

<u>Types of splints</u>
- Rigid or board splint: This splint is the most common and readily available. It comes in different sizes and is adjustable. It consists of stiff boards or plastic and straps so that you can fit and attach the splint to the injured extremity.
- Traction: Used on the legs this type of splint helps reduce pain and encourage circulation by applying a lengthening traction along the limb.
- Air or vacuum: The air splint works as a balloon and the vacuum works by expansion of beads. These splints are both soft and can be wrapped around the extremity and then expanded to provide pressure and immobilization.

Musculoskeletal system injuries

The musculoskeletal system consists of the supporting and protective bones and cartilage of the skeleton and the muscles, tendons and ligaments that connect and move the bones. Tendons attach muscle to bone and ligaments attach bone to bone. Cartilage is the precursor to bone; it is rubbery and flexible. The skeleton of children and infants has a high percentage of cartilage. As we age, the cartilage becomes ossified and turns to bone.

Bones are classified as long, short, flat or irregular. The long bones are those of the limbs and extremities. They tend to be long and thin with a high percentage of compact bone to provide strength. In children, a cartilaginous epiphyseal plate is located close to either end, just below the joint. Long bones have spongy marrow at their ends and down their center where blood supply and nerves are located. The very end of a long bone has smooth cartilage on its surface so it slides easily within its joint.

Short bones are more cubic in shape and can be found in the wrist. Flat bones are protective, encasing bones like the ribs and the skull. Irregular bones are everything else, including the bones in the ear.

Joint injuries include sprains and dislocations that cause tearing and stretching of the tendons and ligaments of the joint. A muscle injury can be a strain, which involves an overextension of the muscle or a tear from overextension or mechanical injury. These types of injury can be open or closed; open means that the skin is broken, closed means the skin has maintained its integrity. The sprained joint will be inflamed and may appear deformed; a dislocated joint will be swollen and deformed. Bruising isn't usually an immediate symptom with these types of injury. Movement may be limited in a sprain or the joint may be frozen in a dislocation.

If there is bleeding of an open injury, this needs to be controlled first. Then splint and apply ice. A shoulder or arm injury should be supported in a sling.

Facial and neck injuries

The priority of an EMT-B in responding to a facial injury is to ensure patency of the airway. The blood supply to the neck and face is extensive and can easily produce an airway blockage from a laceration in the mouth, throat or nose. Because the skull is a strong encasement for the brain, there is reason to suspect internal bleeding if there has been blunt force trauma. Also, damage to the central nervous system and cervical spine are concerns. Fluid emitting from the nose or ears may indicate a skull fracture. Trauma to the throat should be treated as a cervical spine injury, applying a cervical collar as soon as possible.

Important terms

Air embolism: Air within the blood vessels, can be palpated if close to surface.

Subcutaneous emphysema: Air under the skin, can be palpated.

Amputation: Complete removal of an external body part, traumatic or surgical.

Anatomical position: A body standing straight, facing forward, arms at sides with palms turned out; used to define the terms of descriptive anatomy.

Anterior: The front of the body

Avulsion: Tear of tissue from body, may include amputation

Battle's sign: Bruising behind the ears due to head trauma

Compartment syndrome: When a muscle or joint is injured and inflammation is not controlled, pressure within these areas can cut off circulation to the rest of the extremity by swelling to the point where nerves and vessels are occluded.

Compression: A compression injury usually refers to the compression or squeezing together of the vertebrae, causing inflammation of the spinal cord or intervertebral discs.

Contusion: A bruise, bleeding under the skin. A spinal contusion can result in temporary loss of sensation below the injury.

Crepitus: The grinding sound made when the ends of a broken bone rub together.

Cushing's Triad: Three symptoms that there is an increase in pressure around the brain: 1) decreased heart rate, 2) irregular breathing, 3) a widening of the reading between systolic and diastolic blood pressure.

Deep: Far from the surface

Distal: Further from (trunk of body)

Epistaxis: Nosebleed

Evisceration: When an organ, especially abdominal or eyeball, is protruding or sits outside the body.

Flail chest: When a piece of the ribcage breaks away causing the ribcage to expand unevenly, or "flail." It is officially defined as at least two ribs fractured in two or more places, which results in the piece or pieces breaking away.

Frontal plane: A vertical plane that divides the body from anterior and posterior, also called midaxillary or coronal plane.

Golden hour: The sixty-minute period from the point of trauma to the point where surgery is performed, considered crucial in the survival of trauma patients.

Hematoma: A pool or clot of blood under the surface of the skin, within an organ or tissue that causes inflammation.

Inferior: Towards the bottom half

Kinematics: The process of predicting injury patterns by applying the knowledge of physics, anatomy, age, mechanism of injury and preventative safety measures.

Laceration: A cut that penetrates the skin.

Lateral: Far from midline

Medial: Close to center or midline

Midsagittal plane: A vertical plane that divides a body or organ into equal right and left sides; also called midline

Occlusive dressing: Is a dressing that occludes or blocks the entry or exit of air. If applied to a chest wound, only three sides are sealed creating a valve-like action on the open end. When the patient exhales, air can escape but when they inhale the expansion of the chest seals it closed.

Paresthesia: Tingling or numbness of the skin, often called pins and needles.

Paraplegia: Paralysis of both lower limbs.

Pericardial cavity: The membrane lined and fluid filled space that holds the heart. It lies within the thoracic cavity.

Peritoneal cavity: The membrane lined and fluid filled space that holds the organs of the digestive system. It sits below the diaphragm.

Peritoneum: The thin membrane that lines the abdominal and pelvic wall and most of the digestive organs in one continuous sheet. The space it enfolds is called the peritoneal cavity.

Pleural cavity: The membrane lined and fluid filled space that each lung sits in. The pleural cavities sit within the thoracic cavity.

Posterior: The back of the body

Proximal: Closer to (trunk of body)

Raccoon eyes: Bruising around the eyes due to head trauma

Subluxation: When a joint becomes partially dislocated; will involve tearing of ligaments of the joint capsule.

Superficial: Close to the surface

Superior: Towards the head or top half

Transection: Refers to a complete severing of a nerve, vessel, muscle or bone.

Transverse plane: Plane that divides the body from top to bottom, at the belly button

Trendelenburg Position: A surgical or backboard position where the patient is positioned at approximately 45°, with head lower than the torso. Can be used to transport shock patients.

Medical Emergencies

Behavioral call

When a person acts in a way that is not considered normal or appropriate by their family or community, or their actions are not acceptable under normal circumstances it is considered a behavioral emergency.

Many situations can cause altered behavior aside from mental illness. The obvious are drug and alcohol abuse, but hypothermia, hypoglycemia, and shock are all possibilities. When assessing the patient, consider these possibilities when taking history from the patient or bystanders.

An EMT-B called to the scene of a behavioral emergency must first ensure their safety. Consider calling for law enforcement back-up if they are not already on the scene. Be wary of violence or a sudden switch to violent behavior – pacing, shouting and clenching of fists are a good indication that you should be ready to move away quickly. Take a full history from the patient or bystanders. If your local protocol allows, check the patient's blood sugar. If possible, perform an assessment and obtain vital signs. Monitor for sudden changes.

Only one EMT should be in charge of the situation and they should be calm, authoritative and respectful. Communicate with the patient honestly and let them know what is happening in real time. Be patient and compassionate. A patient who refuses care may need to be arrested or restrained.

Refusal of care

An adult may refuse care or refuse to be transported and is within their legal right to do so assuming:
- They are of majority age – 18 + in most states
- They are aware and capable of making informed decisions
- They are not under the influence of drugs or alcohol
- They understand the risks associated with refusing care
- They sign a release form

The adult who has abnormal vital signs or shows signs that their condition will deteriorate should be transported. Help to encourage their decision might come from the medical supervisor, friends and family . If you do leave a patient, be sure to discuss a plan of action with them should their condition deteriorate

"Five rights"

The EMT-B can administer prescribed bronchodilators, nitroglycerin and epinephrine pens in most states. It is also prudent to bring any prescriptions belonging to the patient to the hospital if they are available. The "five rights" of medication administration are a standard safety measure used by medical personnel. They are:
- The right patient
- The right time and frequency
- The right dose
- The right route of administration
- The right drug

These rights are good to keep in mind when documenting incident history.

Drug categories

The following are categories of drugs:
- Opioid analgesics: Painkillers that work by reducing your awareness of the pain; codeine is an opioid analgesic. These are often unintentionally overdosed and are a common cause of drug poisoning; can cause decreased respirations.
- Sedative hypnotics: Slow down body functions. They are commonly known as tranquilizers or sleeping pills. Examples are Valium, Librium, Quaalude and Seconal; may cause decreased respirations.
- Anticholinergics: Impair nerve firing, include antidepressants.
- Cholinergics: An overdose will cause excretion from every orifice.
- Inhalants: Include organic solvents such as airplane glue and paint, nitrites and nitrous oxide. Their effects are fast but brief, although they can cause "instant sniffing death." Solvents act like depressants on the CNS. Nitrites act as vasodilators producing a racing heart and a "rush." Nitrous oxide is known as laughing gas. Inhalants may decrease respiration.
- Sympathomimetics: Imitate adrenalin by increasing heart rate and causing vasoconstriction. They can cause seizures. Includes epinephrine, amphetamine, methamphetamine & cocaine.
- Hallucinogens: Distort thought, senses and perception of time and space. Include "magic mushrooms," LSD and ecstasy.

Hypoglycemia

One of the most common calls for EMS relating to diabetics is for treatment of hypoglycemia (insulin shock). Hypoglycemia occurs when the diabetic has administered insulin and then not followed up with a meal, has used up all their blood glucose with exercise, or the meal has been regurgitated. Basically, the insulin has caused the blood to be drained of energy producing sugar. The brain depends solely on blood sugar; it has no stored energy and so brain function is diminished. The usual protocol is to administer oral glucose. Improvement should be quite rapid. Remember that just because a person is wearing a diabetes medic alert bracelet doesn't mean their symptoms are diabetes related. Always take a history.

Hyperglycemia

Hyperglycemia is when the body is not supplied with insulin. There is no signal to the cells to uptake sugar from the blood and so the cells have to use fatty acids for energy. Fatty acid metabolism produces ketones as a waste product. The ketones build up in the blood and make the blood turn acidic. The ketones can be detected on the breath as a fruity odor. Even the slightest change in pH in the blood can have disastrous effects as all protein structures depend on a stable pH. Hyperglycemic patients need to be hospitalized as soon as possible.

Seizures

A seizure is a short circuit in the brain that is a result of hyperactive firing of a neuron. They can have various causes including trauma, epilepsy and hypoglycemia. A *grand mal seizure* starts with complete loss of consciousness followed by spasm of all the body's muscles. *Petit mal seizures* are also known as *absence seizures*. They are most common in children and last for only a short time (seconds) and are recognized by twitching of the facial muscles or hands. *Focal motor seizures* are isolated muscular quivering or shaking. *Febrile seizures* occur in infants as a result of high fevers.

Treatment is dependent on the severity of the seizure. Loss of consciousness likely involves a fall and so cervical damage should be considered. Oxygen can be administered although this can be difficult to do on a convulsing body. If there is a history of diabetes, administer oral glucose.

Most seizures are over by the time EMS arrives on the scene. Documentation of history and presentation of symptoms is extremely important to expedite treatment upon arrival at the hospital.

Stroke

A stroke is also referred to as a cerebrovascular accident (CVA). It is the result of an interruption of blood circulation in the brain causing death of brain cells. When brain tissue dies, body functions are lost. A stroke will result in paralysis, a loss of speech or loss of sense such as sight. A Transient Ischemic Attack (TIA) is the passing of a blood clot through the brain that results in temporary stroke-like symptoms, including paralysis, numbness and difficulties speaking or understanding. The attack may only last a few minutes or hours. It comes on suddenly and leaves no permanent damage. However, a TIA is a warning that conditions exist for a stroke.

Anaphylaxis

Anaphylaxis is a severe allergic response. In other words, the body over reacts to what it thinks is an invasion. The proteins from insect bites, bee stings, shellfish and nuts frequently illicit this kind of reaction but, anything can cause an anaphylactic response. Symptoms include swelling of the hands or feet, hives, angioedema, decreased blood pressure, coughing and difficulty breathing. The greatest concern is airway management as the swelling can completely close off the throat.

To treat, administer oxygen and perform assessment to determine the severity of the reaction. Look for signs of anaphylactic shock. Also, obtain a focused history to determine possible exposures and if the patient has known allergies. If the patient has an epinephrine injector kit, most states allow you to help administer it. Communicate with medical direction first, and take vital signs before and after the epinephrine has been injected. The epinephrine (adrenalin) works by constricting blood vessels, increasing heart rate and respirations (essentially eliciting the flight or fight response). This treatment will temporarily reduce symptoms until the patient reaches the hospital.

Poisoning

A poison, sometimes called a toxin, is any substance that reacts in the body to cause illness, injury or death. Whether the reaction is physical or psychological it is the body's reaction to a foreign substance interacting with its cells. The result can be anything from a burning sensation to death. Poisons can be inhaled, injected, absorbed and ingested. Some poisonings are instantaneous, like poison ivy, whereas some poisons need to reach a certain level of toxicity before they result in poisonous effects like alcohol.

Substances can enter the body in the following ways:
- Injection: May be directly into a vein, very instantaneous response, seldom accidental
- Ingestion: Eaten, may take up to 6 hours to show effects
- Inhalation: Through the mouth or nose
- Absorption: By contact with the skin or eyes

The procedure for treating poisoning includes the following steps:
- Most important is personal safety. Wear appropriate protective clothing if entering the scene of a contact poisoning. In the case of H_2S or other gas exposure, the EMT must wait for the patient to be retrieved from the contaminated area by trained personnel.
- Ensure and maintain airway, administer high flow O_2 by mask
- Confirm that the symptoms are from a poisoning. This means obtaining a relevant history from a conscious, lucid patient or from bystanders.
- If the poisoning is through contact, flush the contact area as thoroughly as possible with saline or water.
- Under medical direction, if local protocol allows it and the treatment is indicated, an EMT B may be required to administer activated charcoal to absorb the poison or an emetic to induce vomiting.
- Collect any containers or packaging that is associated with the poisoning or bring samples if you can do so without endangering yourself or others. This will help hospital personal determine causes and treatment.

Food poisoning: Most food poisoning comes from bacterial contamination of food which has been left out, improperly processed or exposed to contaminants. E. Coli or Salmonella poisoning are the most common bacteria causing food poisoning and are found in undercooked or exposed meat, poultry, eggs, dairy and seafood. Symptoms include abdominal cramps, nausea, diarrhea and vomiting. There may also be blood in the stool or vomit, or a high fever – these are reasons for possible hospitalization. Dehydration is the major concern.

Poisonous insect and snake bites
- Black widow spider: Small black spider with a red hour glass on abdomen. Bites are rarely fatal but can cause abdominal pain and pain in the muscles of the feet.
- Brown recluse spider: Small brown spider, less than ¾ of an inch long, with a large abdomen, black violin shape on upper portion of the body. Bites may cause a lesion due to digestive juices of spider. Rarely fatal.
- Ticks: Burrow head into skin, usually found on head in the hair. Can carry Lyme disease.
- Rattlesnake (pit viper), copperhead, cottonmouth, coral snake: All require medical attention immediately.
- Black scorpion: Stings through tail, only scorpion poisonous to humans in North America, requires immediate medical attention.
- Any insect or animal bite may cause an anaphylactic response whether they are poisonous or not.

Hypothermia

Hypothermia is when the core body temperature drops below 94°F. However any extreme change in core temperature should be considered serious. Body functions slow down if the body is not at or close to its optimum temperature of 98.6°F.

Hypothermia moves through stages:
- Shivering and complaining of cold
- Shivering stops (below 94°F), skin of torso feels cold
- Mental impairment, slurred speech, loss of balance
- Sleepiness, bradycardia
- Death

Causes of heat loss: Heat loss is due to the natural movement of high energy to low energy; the heat (high energy) of the body is released to something cooler.

- Radiation: The main cause of heat loss, body heat lost to the air in cool temperatures.
- Convection: Body heat is lost to moving air, as in wind, which cools much faster than still air.
- Conduction: Body heat is released to a colder surface by contact. This can be concrete, or water or even wet clothing.
- Evaporation: This is the body's natural means of cooling where the water on the skin evaporates, changing from a liquid to a gas, which requires energy and thus removes heat from the body.
- Respiration: Is really convection as we inhale cool air over our airway, cooling the inside of the body. The air absorbs body heat and releases when we exhale.

Treatment for a hypothermic patient is to prevent any further heat loss by removing wet clothing, wrapping in blankets and removing them from cold surfaces. Do not rewarm a patient unless directed by medical overseer. Treat patient delicately, as whole layers of tissue may be frozen and they are extremely fragile. Frostbite may be an issue. If you are instructed to rewarm frostbitten parts, immerse them in body temperate water. This will be extremely painful for the patient.

Hyperthermia

Hyperthermia is when the core body temperature increases beyond 99°F. Heat cramps are severe cramps in the muscles that result from strenuous activity on a hot day. The body becomes dehydrated and overheats. Treatment is to take the patient out of the heat and provide fluids.

Heat exhaustion is common in seniors who are not used to the heat and are exposed to a sudden increase in temperature. The symptoms include heavy perspiring, nausea and light headiness. Remove the patient to a cooler area and provide oxygen if the patient appears to be showing signs of shock.

Heatstroke can be fatal and may come on without warning. The symptoms can include: hot dry skin, mental confusion, nausea, vomiting and possibly seizures. The body temperature must be lowered immediately by moving the patient to a cooler environment; applying cold packs to the wrists, groin and neck; and even covering with cool wet sheets. Often occurs with seniors.

Suicide

Any threat of suicide should be taken seriously. The most common risk factors for potential suicide are: mood or mental disorders, previous suicide attempts, alcohol or drug abuse. People also at high risk are those who have recently suffered a significant loss, the age groups of 15 to 25 and over 40, and persons who have been talking about suicide and have a suicide plan. Treat as with any behavioral emergency. Communication needs to be direct, compassionate and honest. At the same time, the EMT-B must be automative enough to take control of the situation. These people must be transported, even if they say they have changed their mind. A patient who refuses care may need to be arrested or restrained.

Use of restraints: Some states allow the EMT-B to apply restraints; others require that this is done by law enforcement officers. They should be avoided if at all possible as not only do they change the communication environment between the EMT-B and the patient, but metal hand cuffs and leg irons can cause injury to the joints of the wrist and ankles.

If restraining is required, talk to the conscious patient and explain why you are restraining them and how it will be done. There should be at least 5 personnel to assist – one for each limb and one to put on the restraining straps. Restrain patient to a spinal board in a straightjacket position, so that their arms are crossed in front of their chest, preferably lying on their side. Check distal pulse and respirations regularly on a restrained patient to make sure their circulation hasn't been cut off. If police restraints have been used, remember to bring the associated police officer with you to the receiving facility so they can remove the restraints.

Organic brain syndrome

Organic brain syndrome tends to be a condition of the elderly as it refers to mental dysfunction symptoms that occur within the scope of diseases such as Alzheimer's and Parkinson's as well as resulting from situations such as dementia or multiple strokes.

Overdose

Drug overdose situations can be unpredictable and you may want to have police back-up if you feel there is a potential for violence. Be aware there may be concealed weapons on the body as you do your assessments. Remember that other medical situations including hypothermia, poisoning and hypoglycemia can produce symptoms of severe intoxication. Treat as for a poisoning. Establish airway if necessary and provide oxygen. Transport immediately and monitor vitals regularly. Documentation is essential. Collect any containers that may be associated with the overdose. Get a good relevant history.

Peritonitis

Peritonitis or acute abdomen is the inflammation of the peritoneum. This is usually associated with a digestive organ or vessel that is either bleeding, inflamed or blocked. Acute abdomen may indicate any number of situations including appendicitis, gall bladder infection, duodenal ulcer or ectopic pregnancy.

Symptoms that are associated with peritonitis include:
- Distention of the entire abdomen which may occur from blood, urine, digestive materials or other body fluids leaking into the peritoneal cavity.
- Inflammation and protrusion of the affected organ
- Nausea, vomiting or diarrhea
- Blood in vomit, which may look like coffee grinds
- Blood in stool, which might look black and tarry
- Pain

Acute abdomen

If the patient is conscious and communicating, allow them to find a comfortable position. If load and go is necessary, perform secondary assessment in transport. It is important to limit on-scene time with an acute abdomen condition as it may be the culmination of a serious situation. Do not ignore the possibility of a cardiac situation or pregnancy being the cause. Perform PQRST and ask questions which are pertinent to the pain or inflammation that is presenting. Treat for shock if necessary. Give oxygen if patient may benefit from it. Nothing by mouth! (NPO)

Secondary survey will involve observing the four quadrants of the abdomen, listening for sounds or lack of sound and palpating gently. This may provide an indication of where the pain is and what is causing it. This information can be communicated to the receiving facility.

The EMT-B is not responsible for diagnosing the cause of acute abdomen. Their primary responsibility is to recognize the acute abdomen and transport with care, providing BLS if required.

The most common causes of acute abdomen include:
- Appendicitis: A rupture or inflammation in the appendix which is a bacteria filled organ. Symptoms may present as pain in the right lower quadrant, fever nausea and vomiting.
- Duodenal Ulcer Disease: Ulcers of the stomach. Usually cause a burning or aching pain in the upper half of the abdomen which is brought on by eating acidic foods. Hemorrhaging or perforation will result in acute abdomen symptoms; may present the same as a myocardial infarction.
- Kidney stones: A mineral blockage in the kidneys. May relate to a recent urinary tract infection. Pain is in the lower back and radiates down to the genital area.
- Cholecystitis: Inflammation of the gall bladder or gall stones. Can cause nausea, vomiting and pain in the upper right quadrant of the abdomen. Often occurs after eating fatty foods.
- Pancreatitis: Inflammation of the pancreas often associated with excessive drinking. Symptoms include vomiting and nausea, pain comes from the center of the abdomen and radiates outward.

Referred vs. radiating pain

Radiating pain occurs when a pain starts in one spot and moves outward from that spot. This is a common symptom in myocardial infarction and in back pain. Referred pain is when the pain that is occurring is in a different place than the cause of the pain. The reason that the pain appears elsewhere is because the organ and the spot that the pain is presenting at are innervated by the same nerve. This is common in digestive organs as they work interdependently.

The four quadrants

The abdomen is divided into four quadrants to describe locations when communicating symptoms. The division is down the center, providing right and left side; and transecting across at the navel provides the upper and lower. The distribution of organs is as follows:
- Upper Right: Liver, gallbladder, top of pancreas, right kidney, part of duodenum, part of colon.
- Upper Left: Spleen, end of pancreas, stomach, left kidney, part of colon
- Lower Right: Appendix, ascending colon, small intestine, right ovary and fallopian tube.
- Lower Left: Small intestine, descending colon, left ovary.

Drowning

The following are considerations in drowning or near drowning incidents:
- Hypothermia: Remove wet clothing and keep the patient warm. A severely hypothermic patient may appear dead.
- Spinal injury: Always assume a spinal or cervical injury has occurred
- Personal safety: Only personnel fully trained in water rescue should attempt to retrieve a drowning victim from the water.
- AED: Make sure patient is dry before using the AED.

Genital injuries

Genital injuries are treated the same as an abdominal or soft tissue injury. Bleeding should be controlled first, followed by ice to reduce inflammation. Do not attempt to remove impaled objects. Do not attempt to replace avulsed tissue. If possible, have the same gender EMT work with the patient.

Sexual assault

Considerations in dealing with sexual assault victims:
- Ensure the police are on the scene
- Same gender EMT should work with the victim
- Be careful not move, remove or destroy any evidence unless necessary to provide treatment.
- Document carefully and take good notes as you might have to appear in court.
- Use professional, supportive manner, do not pass judgment.
- Advise the patient not to douche, wash, brush teeth, urinate or have a bowel movement until seen by police and a physician.

Important terms

Angioedema: A puffiness of face, lips and neck due swelling underneath the skin; common in allergic reactions.

Aura: The state of mind just before onset of a seizure; strange feeling, some may experience visions

Diabetes type-I: Juvenile diabetes requires daily insulin injection

Diabetes type-II: Adult onset diabetes, can be controlled by diet, exercise and weight loss

Dysarthria: Slurred speech

Expressive aphasia: Loss of speech

Hemorrhagic stroke: Rupture of a blood vessel in the brain.

Hyperglycemia: High blood sugar

Hypoglycemia: Low blood sugar

Insulin: Hormone produced by the pancreas that regulates glucose metabolism (blood sugar) by signaling the cells of the body to intake sugar from the blood.

Ischemic stroke: A blocking of an artery of the brain which prevents blood flow and oxygen to brain tissue, usually caused by atherosclerosis. This is the most common type of stroke.

Ketoacidosis: A lowering of blood pH due to the use of fatty acids for energy. This happens when insulin is not present to allow glucose to enter the cells. It is usually associated with hyperglycemia.

Postictal: After seizure state, brain is recovering. Patient is likely confused and exhausted.

Receptive aphasia: Loss of understanding

Status epilepticus: When seizures come one on top of the other, so that there is more than 3 per hour or they last progressively longer. This is a medical emergency.

Obstetrics and Pediatrics

Anatomy

The following anatomy terms regarding obstetrics:
- Fetus: The baby itself.
- Amniotic sac: A fluid-filled sac that holds the fetus; provides protection; usually breaks by itself in the first stage of labor
- Placenta: The organ that provides a blood supply and waste removal system for fetus.
- Umbilical cord: Connects baby to placenta.
- Mucous plug: At the cervix, providing a protective seal. Often passing of the mucous plug is the first sign of labor.

Special situations

The following are special situations that occur during pregnancy:
- Tubal pregnancy: Occurs when the egg is fertilized and implants itself within the fallopian tube rather than in the uterus (also known as an ectopic pregnancy). Usually, there is rupture of the tube within the first few weeks, causing major bleeding.
- Umbilical cord prolapse: Umbilical cord first. This is an emergency, transport immediately keeping mother in a position so that her hips are higher than her head.
- Breech birth: Buttocks first. This is an emergency; transport immediately keeping mother in a position so that her hips are higher than her head. Umbilical cord prolapse is common in breech presentation.
- Limb presentation: When an arm or leg shows first, often called breech birth also. Treat as a breech birth.

Stages of labor

There are three stages of labor:
1. Contractions begin; cervix dilates and thins, making room for baby's head. May take anywhere from a few minutes to several hours.
2. Baby moves down the birth canal and is delivered. Usually takes one or two hours.
3. Placenta is delivered. Usually takes about 10 minutes to an hour.

Imminent birth

You know you will have to deliver the baby if:
- You can see the head or an outline of the head against the perineum.
- Contractions are between 2 and 3 minutes apart.
- Mother has the urge to push.

Labor will progress faster with a mother who has had one or more normal deliveries. Transport should be initiated at the first sign of complication; communication with medical director should be maintained at all times.

Steps you should take to prepare for an imminent birth:
- Universal precautions should be taken prior to contact.
- Position mother on her back with her knees up and apart. Place towels under her buttocks to elevate them slightly.
- Line the area around the vagina with sheets, paper towels or blankets to create as sterile environment as possible.
- When the head is presenting, place your gloved hand on it, careful not to press on the fontanel but directing enough firmness to deal with an explosive delivery should it occur.

Steps from head presentation to delivery:
- Your hand should support the head from the back to help prevent over extension of the neck. Careful, wet babies are very slippery.
- If amniotic sac has not broken use a clamp to tear it and then gently pull it away from the baby's nose and mouth.
- Use a bulb to suction baby's mouth and then nose.
- Check for umbilical cord around the neck. If it is there, try to unwrap it by sliding it over the head or over the shoulder. If it needs to be cut, place two clamps on the cord about two inches apart and then cut between the clamps. If there is bleeding from the cord after cutting, try adding another clamp.
- Allow the rest of the baby to be delivered.

Steps after delivery
- Once the baby is delivered wrap it in blankets and lay it on its side near the mother's vagina, with its head lower than feet to encourage drainage. Suction nose and mouth again.
- Protocols differ here as to when to cut umbilical cord, pulsating or after it stops. Either way, cutting the cord requires clamping it with two clamps about 6 and 8 inches from where it attaches to the baby. Cut between the clamps.
- Record time of delivery.
- When placenta is delivered, keep it clean and transport it with baby and mother.
- Massage uterus by placing your hand on the mother's lower abdomen and massaging with extended fingers.
- Perform APGAR on baby.

APGAR score
The APGAR score is a rating system to standardize the assessment of a newborn baby by rating appearance, pulse, grimace, activity and respirations on a scale of 0 to 2.

Appearance:
- Pale or blue – 0 points
- Pink torso – 1 point
- Pink all over 2 points

Pulse:
- No pulse – 0 points
- Pulse under 100 bpm – 1 point
- Pulse 100 bpm or more 2 points

Grimace:
- No reflexive facial grimace when you flick their feet – 0 points
- Slight grimace – 1 point
- Cough, cry or grimace – 2 points

Activity:
- No movement – 0 points
- Slight movement of hands and feet – 1 point
- Active – 2 points

Respirations:
- No respiration – 0
- Slow or irregular – 1 point
- Normal with crying – 2 points

The scoring should be done 1 minute and 5 minutes after the baby is born. If score is less than 4, resuscitation should be instigated immediately. A rating of 4-6 indicates the baby needs immediate medical attention. The score from 7-10 is a normal.

Miscarriage

Miscarriage, also called spontaneous abortion, is the unplanned ending of a pregnancy that is 20 weeks along or less. The signs may range from pinky discharge to contractions and hemorrhaging. Initiate load and go. Collect any "products of conception" or tissue that has been discharged if possible. Keep tissue clean and dry in a plastic bag and transport them with the patient.

Miscarriage should be treated as a loss. The EMT needs to be emotionally supportive. Use the term miscarriage in communication; "spontaneous abortion" has negative implications to many people. Avoid letting the patient or family see any of the collected tissues.

Monitor the patient for signs of shock and treat accordingly. Otherwise, the patient can be transported on her left side, use appropriate amount of absorbent pads at the vaginal opening.

Vaginal bleeding during pregnancy

Vaginal bleeding during pregnancy is considered an emergency; the further along the pregnancy, the greater the emergency and the patient should be transported. Spotting during early pregnancy is not uncommon, nor is a very small amount of bleeding in other stages. If there is excessive bleeding, with or without cramping, monitor for signs of shock and transport the patient immediately. Replace the sanitary pads regularly. Bring all used pads to the hospital for examination. Transport patient lying on their left side.

Pregnancy terms

Eclampsia (also called toxemia): Seizures or coma resulting from high blood pressure induced by pregnancy (preeclampsia). It can occur during pregnancy or up to 24 hours after birth.

Meconium: First bowel movement of an infant, usually black or green and tarry.

Meconium aspiration is a concern during delivery if meconium is released before birth in the amniotic sac, as this can cause airway blockage.

Preeclampsia: High blood pressure during pregnancy that leads to severe headaches, blurred vision and puffiness in hands and feet from kidney dysfunction.

Pediatric patients

Considerations in dealing with pediatric patients:
- Children and infants are smaller and have a much higher metabolism than adults. This is a major consideration as they tend to bleed out faster, dehydrate faster, overheat faster and cool down faster than adults.
- Children breathe using their abdominal muscles and diaphragm muscles rather than chest muscles until about 8 years old. Care must be taken not to restrict their breathing by restricting their abdomen movement.
- The airway in a child is much softer and can be easily collapsed or damaged. Their tongues are larger than the airway and mouth and can easily block the airway.
- The bones of a child are softer. They can take more bend during trauma however this also means that internal organs can take a lot of damage that may not show due to flexibility of the ribcage.
- Children have less fat around their organs and so they are much more susceptible to organ injury with abdominal trauma.

Age subsets of pediatrics:
- Neonate: Less than 4 weeks, no concern when approached
- Infant: From 4 weeks to 1 year, no concern when approached, may want to stay in parents arms
- Toddler: 1-3 years, separation anxiety, assess across the room first, work from toe to head, keep child on parents lap
- Preschooler: 3-6 years, keep with parent, talk to them about what you are doing, let them help, examine toe to head.
- School-age: 6-12 years, talk to them directly then to their parent, head to toe, allow them to answer some questions but realize that answers may be imaginative.
- Adolescent: 12-18 years, may want to be examined privately away from parent so they can be honest, treat as adults but be firm if they are uncooperative. Best to have same gender EMT.

Pediatric assessment triangle: Pediatric assessment triangle is an assessment used by EMS personnel to assess children by their appearance before making any physical contact. It is often called the "across the room assessment." Essentially, the idea is to assess the patient before your actual presence causes a change in their behavior. The three sides to the triangle are:
- Appearance: Does the child appear well? Good muscle tone, normal cry and responsiveness?
- Work of breathing: Is the child breathing normally or working to breathe?
- Circulation: Is the child's color good? Are they bleeding?

Any abnormal observations are cause to contact ALS or for immediate transport.

Family considerations: Dealing with the family of a child in an emergency situation can be a situation in itself. A normal response to seeing the child suffering may be near hysteria. It is wise to call for back up to deal with the family if you feel you are overwhelmed. Remain calm, confident and professional. Communicate with the family using the child's name and making eye contact. If there is a language barrier, see if a neighbor or relative can help translate.

The child will likely be calmer if a parent is kept close by at all times; this may include transporting the baby in the parent's arms. If the child is chronically ill, the parent may have specific information on treatment. Don't hesitate to communicate with them. Ask open ended questions when assessing the scene and the patient. Document meticulously.

Abuse and neglect

Abuse is any extreme or inappropriate behavior or action or lack thereof that results in harm to another. Neglect is a form of abuse where the dependent, in this case a child, is not receiving adequate attention or care.

If an EMT is called to a home where a youngster is found alone, the EMT can suspect neglect. If the child is looking thin, excessively unkempt, or has a need for medical attention that has not been seen to, an EMT should report it to the authorities. Regular calls to the same home, injuries or explanations of injuries that don't make sense also need to be reported. An EMT should never make accusations or imply they suspect something; this is not in their scope of practice. Careful documentation and reporting are the best course of action.

SIDS

SIDS stands for sudden infant death syndrome, the sudden and unexplained death of an infant under one year of age. Very often the EMT is the first on the scene and this is a very traumatic situation. The EMT needs to be calm and professional. The parents will be a major concern in a situation like this and you might need to call for back up to help you with them. Many states will require you to begin resuscitative methods even if signs of death are obvious. Careful observation of the scene and documentation of your observations and actions are crucial.

Geriatrics

GEMS diamond

The GEMS diamond is a mnemonic used to remember the issues important in assessing a senior patient.

- **G**: Stands for geriatric, referring to elderly patients. They are different physiologically and psychologically.
- **E**: Consider their environment: Is it warm? Clean? Safe? Are they caring for themselves or being cared for sufficiently?
- **M**: Do they have any significant medical conditions? Are they on medications?
- **S**: Is there a social support network in place? Are they getting some contact with people? Do they have family and friends checking on them?

Physiology in geriatric patients

The main causes of physiological aging are a result of a reduced number of cells in the body. Many cells reach a certain age and stop dividing. Effects include:
- Skin changes: The epidermis is thinner and more delicate, the dermis is less flexible.
- Musculoskeletal: The bones become smaller and more brittle, especially with osteoporosis; muscle size is reduced, making them slower and weaker.
- Brain cells decrease in number: Causes slower responses and less acute senses.
- Heart muscle becomes weaker: Results in less volume of blood being pumped throughout the body.
- Kidneys become smaller and have less blood flow: Results in reduced blood filtering capability, more waste in blood, less in urine.
- Collagen hardening: Collagen, a major connective tissue fiber, crosslinks more and more as we age which results in stiffening of arteries, muscles, joints and less resiliency of the skin.
- Digestive processes slow: Smooth muscles are weaker and blood flow is reduced to digestive organs.

DNR

DNR stands for Do Not Resuscitate. Check local protocol. A person over the age of 18 has a right to have a DNR order, otherwise known as an advanced directive or living will. It means that they have made the choice to not have CPR performed on them should they experience respiratory or cardiac failure. In most states, the order needs to be signed by the person's physician. It can be a document or in the form of a bracelet or necklace.

If in doubt, always start CPR. DNR does not mean that the patient doesn't receive care in making them comfortable and this can include oxygen, intravenous fluids and medication.

Elder abuse

Elder abuse is becoming more and more prominent as the baby boomer population ages and the senior population becomes larger. It can be physical, emotional, sexual or financial. It is most often seen in seniors over 80 who have increasing medical problems and often have dementia. An EMT may see it when assessing the environment the elder is living in: lack of food, improper clothing, unexplained trauma, lack of medication or basic needs such as dentures or glasses.

Abuse can occur in nursing homes or when an elder is left to live alone when they are not capable of caring for themselves. All abuse should be reported immediately.

Dementia & delirium

Dementia is from the Latin word meaning irrational. Dementia is a mental condition that may result from many diseases, and is commonly associated with Alzheimer's disease. It is a progressive deterioration of mental function including disorientation, confusion, loss of reason and deterioration of memory and intellect.

Delirium is a sudden onset of confused and disordered mental capacity that can include inability to communicate and hallucinations. It can be caused by illness, dehydration, or medications. It is more common in hospitalized geriatric patients.

Geriatric considerations

In dealing with seniors, one should keep in mind that:
- They may be slower at responding, for no other reason than they are *old*.
- They may expect to be treated with a formality that isn't used with other populations.
- They may or may not be hard of hearing, presuming they are may be insulting.
- You must determine what the complaint was that elicited the EMS call. If you simply ask them what is wrong, you may not get a direct answer, often they have many things wrong.
- They are prone to depression.
- Memories aren't always sharp.
- Differences in physiology and the effects of medications may cause a condition to present differently in an elderly person, especially heart rate and blood pressure symptoms.

Important terms

Kyphosis: Severe curvature of the back resulting in a hunchback appearance. This posture can inhibit breathing and digestion.

Polypharmacy: The use of five or more prescribed or over the counter drugs by a patient. This can include herbal medicines. It is often the result of seeing more than one physician or taking supplements. The interactions of the medications can cause serious complications.

Spondylosis: Degeneration of the spine that causes stiffening and immobility.

Operations

Patient assessment process

The order of patient assessment process from the point where you arrive on scene to the point of transport is as follows:
1. Scene Survey
2. Initial assessment: airway, breathing, circulation.
3. SAMPLE history and focused physical exam
4. Detailed physical exam (if applicable)
5. Ongoing assessment – monitor vital signs every five minutes, repeat detailed physical exam if condition changes.

Load and go can be initiated at any time during the patient assessment.

Run report

The run report or pre-hospital care report is a written legal and medical document. These documents should be carefully recorded for your protection as well as the patient's. All events and the time they occurred should be reported accurately and legibly. If a mistake is made in the document, put a line through the mistake, then date and initial the correction. Record data as it occurs. Falsifying a report is a legal offense and also puts the patient in danger. These are confidential reports that should not be seen by the public. A verbal report can be delivered as you deliver the patient to the receiving facility. The complete written report must be completed before returning to duty.

Two-way radios

The two-way radio can be mobile or portable. Important points to remember when using the radio are:
- Always ensure batteries are charged at the beginning of your shift.
- Don't hold down the button unless you have something ready to say.
- Use terminology, codes and abbreviations that local EMS use, take time to learn the proper language.
- The two-way radio system (citizen's band radio) is public, anyone can listen. Be professional.
- Know local protocols regarding what is acceptable information to transmit.
- Be brief and speak clearly.

Truck check

At the beginning of every shift, the truck should be inspected. There should be a systematic protocol in place that includes the following check points:
- Truck fluid levels topped up, check radiator for leaks, look under vehicle for leaks
- Flashers and lights all working order
- Check wipers for operation, doors.
- Test park break.
- Check tire pressure
- Adjust mirrors, seats for current operator
- Cell phone and radio batteries should be replaced with freshly charged ones at the beginning of a shift.
- Radio check is performed on both the mobile radio and portable radios, confirming their function with dispatch
- Perform medical supply/equipment check

Following a checklist, one should ensure:
- Listed medical supplies are all stocked in truck
- Pharmaceuticals stocked and expiration dates checked
- Batteries on AED, cardiac monitor and all portable operating equipment are checked and replaced if needed
- Oxygen tanks should be inspected for leaks and regulator issues. Make sure they are adequately full
- Disposable equipment such as tubing, masks and artificial airways are stocked up
- Required forms, papers and pens are in the truck ready for documentation

Ambulance operations

Depending on local regulations, the driver needs to be licensed appropriately and have training to drive an emergency vehicle. There should be at least two qualified personnel per ambulance, one to drive and one to perform patient care. Drivers need to be able to communicate over the radio and make decisions regarding the appropriate route to take, which means being familiar with the operational area. They also need to know the appropriate use of lights and sirens as regulated by their jurisdiction. At a call, the ambulance should always be parked at a safe distance from the scene: uphill from leaks and at least 100 feet, or a safe distance from the wreckage of an accident. Headlights can be turned off and warning lights left on. Make sure to park in a place that allows you to exit quickly and safely without being blocked or blocking other emergency vehicles.

Post run procedures

Communicate with dispatch when you arrive at the station. Post run priority is to complete the written pre-hospital report and any other documentation and submit them. Retrieve information from dispatch that might be needed to make the report as accurate as possible. Report should be filed immediately in a secure place. The ambulance and equipment must be thoroughly cleaned and disinfected using proper disinfecting soap as per local protocols. Be sure that the soap is not expired.

Restock equipment as necessary. Check oxygen tanks and replace if necessary. Check AED battery and radio battery for charge. Refuel truck. Communicate with dispatch when ambulance is ready to run again.

Communication with dispatch

The times you should communicate with dispatch while responding to a call include:
- To confirm call by repeating location back to dispatcher
- Upon your arrival at the scene; communicate any discrepancies between dispatch and the scene, for instance, wrong address.
- If there are more patients than you can deal with
- If you require police assistance
- If you require ALS
- To communicate with medical director as necessary
- When en route to let them know where you are going
- Upon arrival at receiving facility
- When you leave the receiving facility
- When you arrive at your station
- When the truck is ready to run

Lifting and carrying

It is important to pay attention to the following when lifting and carrying:
- Never lift more than you are capable of lifting, call for help if you need it.
- Keep back straight, abdominal muscles engaged
- Lift from the legs, bending the knees
- Never lift with extended arms or back
- Never lift and twist
- Work as a team, follow the team leader's direction
- Keep feet hip width apart

Patient moves

The types of moves used are dependent on the stability of the scene that the patient is found in and the stability of the patient themselves.

- Emergency: Emergency extrication is required when the patient and the EMT are at risk and both must get out of the immediate vicinity quickly. In this case, moving the patient as quickly as possible is more important than securing the neck with a cervical collar. Instances where this would apply would be poisonous gas leaks or fire.
- Urgent: An urgent move would be used in a circumstance where the patient must be transported quickly because they are unstable, but it will not risk their lives to take the time to put on a cervical collar.
- Nonurgent: Nonurgent moves are used when the patient can be stabilized at the scene before transfer.

Patient-transfer

Types of equipment used to transfer patients in a pre-hospital setting:
- Wheeled ambulance stretcher: Stretcher with a wheeled base that can be lowered so that it slides into the ambulance
- Stair chair: A chair with wheels and wheelbarrow style handles that can be used to move patients where a wheeled ambulance stretcher will not be safe. Not for use with suspected spinal injuries.
- Scoop stretcher: A type of stretcher that can be broken into 2 or 4 pieces and slid together under the patient

Positioning of patient during transport: Patients can be placed in the following positions during transport, depending on the patient's situation:
- Trendelenburg (flat on back with gurney angled so that head is lower than feet): For suspected spinal injury
- Shock position (on back with feet elevated): If patient is in shock and there is no indication of spinal injury
- Supine (on back): Suspected neck or pelvic injury
- Semi-fowler's (head elevated): If patient is having difficulty breathing or chest pain, no indication of spinal injury.
- Left side: When patient is not unconscious, especially a pregnant woman, no indication of spinal injury

When transporting the patient, it is important to use safety restraints. One should be placed just below the armpits across the chest and under the arms; the other should be placed across the thighs.

Practice Test

Questions 1 to 3 pertain to the following scenario:
> You and your partner are called to the home of a 75-year-old man complaining of severe pain in the chest and nausea. As the patient is being assessed, he suddenly loses consciousness.

1. The first step in treating a patient with severe chest pain is:
   a. obtain a patient history.
   b. administer oxygen.
   c. perform a physical exam.
   d. obtain baseline vital signs.

2. The first step in treating a patient who loses consciousness is to:
   a. obtain a pulse.
   b. assess breathing.
   c. attach an automated external defibrillator.
   d. open the airway.

3. The best way to decrease oxygen demand in the case of cardiac compromise is to:
   a. transport the patient immediately, flashing lights and using siren.
   b. reassure the patient.
   c. travel at high speed but without the siren.
   d. give the patient nitroglycerin.

Questions 4 to 6 pertain to the following scenario:
> You receive a call from the mother of a 3-year-old girl. The mother believes her daughter has "swallowed something." When you arrive, the child does not acknowledge your presence. She has a high fever and a generalized rash.

4. Proper care for a small child with possible airway obstruction consists of:
   a. performing a finger sweep.
   b. relieving mild airway obstruction.
   c. avoiding agitation of the child and providing transport.
   d. applying back blows and abdominal thrusts.

5. When a young child does not acknowledge the presence of a stranger in his or her environment, this is indicative of:
   a. altered mental state.
   b. allergic reaction.
   c. sleep.
   d. age-appropriate behavior.

6. A child with inattentive behavior, high fever, and generalized rash should be monitored for:
   a. dehydration.
   b. projectile vomiting.
   c. cardiac failure.
   d. seizures.

7. In which of the following patients is rapid trauma assessment most urgently needed?
   a. A 90-year-old woman with pain in the right upper quadrant.
   b. A conscious 50-year-old man who fell from the roof of his home and landed on his left arm.
   c. A conscious 25-year-old store clerk who was stabbed in the abdomen during an attempted robbery.
   d. An 8-year-old boy complaining of pain in the right lower quadrant of the abdomen.

8. You receive a call from a young woman whose car has been struck in a shopping mall parking lot. She is concerned about the elderly man who backed into her car. On arrival at the scene, you find a conscious 88-year-old man who appears to be having an acute ischemic stroke. The most appropriate course of action would be to:
   a. perform a physical exam.
   b. administer oxygen and obtain a patient history.
   c. monitor blood pressure.
   d. administer oxygen and provide transport to the hospital for fibrinolytic therapy.

Questions 9 and 10 refer to the following scenario:
   The husband of a pregnant 21-year-old woman calls for assistance, fearing that his wife is about to deliver "any minute." On arrival, delivery does not appear to be imminent; however, during transport, crowning occurs.

9. The most appropriate course of action is to:
   a. check for the presence of the amniotic sac.
   b. reassure the mother and wait for arrival at the hospital.
   c. apply gentle pressure to the infant's head.
   d. gently slide the infant back into the birth canal.

10. On delivery, the infant is not breathing adequately and the umbilical cord is pulsating. You should immediately:
    a. pull on the umbilical cord.
    b. leave the umbilical cord attached until arrival at the hospital.
    c. clamp and cut the umbilical cord.
    d. clamp the umbilical cord and await arrival at the hospital.

Questions 11 to 13 pertain to the following scenario:
   The manager of a fast-food restaurant calls to report that an elderly woman is choking. On arrival, you find an 80-year-old woman in a wheelchair in obvious respiratory distress. On breathing assessment, you observe that the patient's dentures are loose and ill-fitting. She then begins to make gurgling sounds.

11. The first step in evaluating the airway of an elderly person is to:
    a. extend the head and flex the neck.
    b. thrust the jaw forward to pull the tongue out of the airway.
    c. find a radial pulse.
    d. suction for 30 seconds.

12. While evaluating the airway, you notice there may be some difficulty in ventilating the patient. You should proceed by:
    a. removing the patient's dentures.
    b. suctioning for 30 seconds.
    c. initiating the gag reflex.
    d. offering high-concentration oxygen.

13. The presence of gurgling sounds in this patient indicates that:
    a. the patient is in cardiac arrest.
    b. the patient is in an altered mental state.
    c. the patient requires suctioning.
    d. the patient is having an acute ischemic attack.

14. You arrive at the home of a 75-year-old woman who has had a fall. In addition to assessing potential injuries, you should:
    a. assess mental status.
    b. oxygenate the patient.
    c. assess potential causes of the fall.
    d. assess circulation.

15. Which of the following drugs are most often carried on an ambulance?
    a. Nitroglycerin
    b. Epinephrine
    c. Inhalers
    d. Oral glucose

16. Which of the following drugs can an EMT-B assist a patient in taking?
    a. Nitroglycerin
    b. Amitriptyline
    c. Verapamil
    d. Nifedipine

Questions 17 to 19 pertain to the following scenario:
You are called to the scene of a traffic accident involving a mother and her 2-year-old son. On arrival, both mother and child are bleeding from the head. The mother is conscious and alert and informs you that while she has sustained "just a scratch," her son is "seriously hurt." The boy has a laceration on the top of his head. On examination, he exhibits signs of hypoperfusion.

17. One of the most common causes of hypoperfusion in infants and children is:
    a. heart failure.
    b. blood loss.
    c. a stressful event.
    d. lack of oxygen.

18. Which of the following is a sign of hypoperfusion in children?
    a. Crying.
    b. Rapid pulse.
    c. Rapid respiratory rate.
    d. Increased urinary output.

19. The best course of care for this child is to:
    a. wait for signs of decompensated shock.
    b. perform airway clearance.
    c. monitor blood pressure.
    d. keep the child warm.

20. The most likely cause of cardiac arrest in a child is:
    a. respiratory failure.
    b. hypothermia.
    c. mitral valve prolapse.
    d. asthma attack.

Questions 21 to 23 pertain to the following scenario:

The morning after a snow storm, the ski patrol discover the wreckage of an automobile on the road to a ski lodge. A 70-year-old man is trapped inside. He is disoriented but conscious and has suffered a broken hip. He exhibits severe muscular rigidity and has no memory of the events before or after the accident. The patient's wife had reported the man missing the previous night after he became intoxicated and was ejected from a local bar.

21. In addition to a broken hip, this patient is suffering from:
    a. hypoperfusion.
    b. inadequate circulation.
    c. hypothermia.
    d. psychiatric disorder.

22. To prevent heat loss in an injured patient, you should:
    a. perform active rewarming techniques.
    b. massage the extremities.
    c. administer a stimulant.
    d. use blankets to provide a barrier to the outside.

23. Body heat loss is often associated with:
    a. alcohol intoxication.
    b. head trauma.
    c. cardiac events.
    d. altered mental status.

24. The signs and symptoms of carbon monoxide poisoning most closely resemble those of:
    a. smoke inhalation.
    b. flu.
    c. food poisoning.
    d. drug overdose.

25. You receive an urgent call from the mother of a 15-year-old-boy who has accidentally splashed disinfectant in his eye while performing his weekly chore of cleaning the bathroom. The best way to treat the boy is to
    a. irrigate the eye with clean water for 20 minutes if an alkali or 10 minutes if an acid.
    b. irrigate the eye with diluted vinegar.
    c. irrigate the eye with baking soda and water.
    d. transport the patient to the hospital immediately.

Questions 26 to 28 pertain to the following scenario:

You receive a call from a distraught 18-year-old girl. Her parents are away for the weekend and she is having an illicit party during which alcohol and other substances have been consumed. Her 16-year-old brother has slipped and hit his head on the coffee table. The boy has a contusion on the side of his head. He is conscious but has slurred speech and appears confused. He denies having consumed any alcohol or drugs.

26. In addition to alcohol intoxication, slurred speech and confusion may be signs of:
    a. altered mental state.
    b. head injury.
    c. seizure.
    d. drug overdose.

27. The best course of action in this case would be to:
    a. transport the patient to the hospital.
    b. call the police.
    c. ask the patient again if he has been using drugs.
    d. call the parents.

28. The patient suddenly becomes violent and begins to throw objects around the room. Your reaction should be to:
    a. reassure the patient.
    b. restrain the patient.
    c. go to a safe place and call the police.
    d. call the parents.

29. Which of the following indicates correct placement of an endotracheal tube?
    a. Presence of breath sounds only in the epigastrium
    b. Presence of breath sounds on the right apex
    c. Presence of breath sounds on the left apex
    d. Presence of breath sounds on both the right and left

30. Which of the following does **not** affect the accuracy of an oximeter reading?
    a. Cigarette smoking
    b. Hypothermia
    c. Carbon monoxide poisoning
    d. Fever

Questions 31 to 33 pertain to the following scenario:
    The wife of a 65-year-old man calls, fearing that her husband is "having a heart attack." When you arrive, the man is conscious, but sweating profusely and complaining of chest pain. He tells you the pain developed while he was mowing the lawn. When asked if he is taking any medications, he says he has been on nitroglycerin, and that although he took the "maximum dose," it did not alleviate the chest pain. After taking his vital signs, you observe that his pulse is 130 beats per minute and blood pressure is 200/100. The patient gives you permission to transport him to the hospital.

31. According to SAMPLE, the information you should always obtain from patient includes:
    a. medication history.
    b. insurance information.
    c. physician's name.
    d. emergency contact information.

32. Profuse sweating in a patient is an example of a
    a. symptom.
    b. sign.
    c. drug overdose.
    d. medication side effect.

33. Nitroglycerin is often prescribed for patients with:
    a. congestive heart failure.
    b. clogged arteries.
    c. angina pectoris.
    d. arrhythmia.

34. Compared with adults, infants and children have:
    a. slower pulse.
    b. higher blood pressure.
    c. slower respiratory rate.
    d. lower blood pressure.

35. You are called to the home of a 75-year-old woman who has stopped breathing. Her husband requests that you do not resuscitate the patient because she has terminal cancer. Your procedure should include:
    a. not resuscitate the patient as her husband requests.
    b. contact medical direction.
    c. try to resuscitate the patient.
    d. transport the patient to the hospital.

36. While off duty, you observe a severe car accident, with one of the vehicles overturned. Your procedure should include:
    a. provide care to the victims, then leave the scene.
    b. provide care and wait for additional help to arrive.
    c. call 911 and leave the scene.
    d. begin care, call for additional help, then leave the scene.

37. Which of the following is **not** useful in assessing an unresponsive adult patient with head trauma?
    a. Mental status
    b. Airway obstruction
    c. Capillary refill
    d. Skin color

38. A dangerous pulse rate for an adult in an emergency situation would be:
    a. above 100 beats per minute.
    b. below 50 beats per minute.
    c. 60 beats per minute.
    d. 90 beats per minute.

39. A pulse rate of 120 beats per minute in a 3-year-old child is
    a. not a cause for concern.
    b. indicative of imminent cardiac arrest.
    c. indicative of accidental drug overdose.
    d. indicative of shock.

40. You have difficulty in finding the carotid pulse of an injured 5-year-old girl. You should:
    a. use your thumb.
    b. apply more pressure.
    c. assess the carotid pulse on the other side.
    d. assess the carotid pulse on both sides.

Questions 41 to 43 pertain to the following scenario:
You are called to the scene of a traffic accident involving a 40-year-old woman. The patient is conscious but reports that her airbag deflated and she was thrown against the steering wheel. You notice a large cut on her forehead and bruising on her neck.

41. Because of her injuries, this patient is at risk of :
    a. shock.
    b. cervical spine injury.
    c. subdural hematoma.
    d. internal bleeding.

42. The first step in treating this patient is to:
    a. manually stabilize the head and neck.
    b. apply a soft collar.
    c. apply a rigid collar.
    d. secure the patient to a backboard.

43. Before you transport this patient to the hospital, you should:
    a. apply a soft collar.
    b. apply a rigid collar.
    c. palpate the back of the neck.
    d. tilt the head back.

44. A detailed physical examination is most often performed on:
    a. an accident victim with a broken leg.
    b. an elderly patient with a heart condition.
    c. an accident victim with head trauma.
    d. a child with airway obstruction.

45. In the case of a patient with chronic bronchitis in respiratory distress, the preferred course of action is to:
    a. withhold oxygen.
    b. provide artificial ventilation.
    c. place the patient in a supine position.
    d. administer oxygen.

Questions 46 to 48 pertain to the following scenario:
You receive a call from the wife of a 66-year-old man with COPD. The man has been having difficulty breathing. When you arrive, he is making gurgling sounds and cannot speak. He appears disoriented and his skin is flushed.

46. Gurgling sounds in a patient with breathing difficulty are usually a sign of:
    a. open airway.
    b. obstruction.
    c. fluid in throat.
    d. stridor.

47. The typical position for COPD patients with breathing difficulty is:
    a. sitting with feet dangling.
    b. tripod position.
    c. lying down.
    d. hunching over.

48. Altered mental status in a patient who has difficulty breathing is usually a sign of:
   a. COPD.
   b. airway obstruction.
   c. lack of oxygen.
   d. cyanosis.

Questions 49 to 51 pertain to the following scenario:
   A 38-year-old woman falls through the ice while skating on a frozen pond with her 6-year-old daughter. While the child went to get help, her mother had been trapped waist-deep in the freezing water for several hours. After rescue, the woman reports that her toes are freezing. On assessment, her toes appear grayish-blue in color and feel frozen to the touch.

49. The first step in caring for this patient would be to:
   a. squeeze the toes to increase circulation.
   b. perform active rewarming.
   c. massage the toes to increase circulation.
   d. administer high-concentration oxygen.

50. Transport to the hospital has been severely delayed due to icy road conditions. A rescue worker offers the patient a drink of an alcoholic beverage from a flask to keep her warm. The next step in treating this patient should be to:
   a. continue to massage the frozen area.
   b. begin active rewarming.
   c. heat a container of water and immerse the patient's feet until they touch the bottom.
   d. keep the frozen area covered and allow the patient to sip the alcoholic beverage.

51. In the process of active rewarming, you should:
   a. put pressure on the affected area to rapidly increase circulation.
   b. allow the patient to walk on the affected area to increase circulation.
   c. keep the affected area immersed until the patient feels pain.
   d. keep the affected area wrapped in blankets until transport is available.

52. In rescuing a near-drowning victim, you should:
   a. perform chest compression.
   b. attempt rescue breathing while the victim is still in the water.
   c. remove the victim from the water before initiating care.
   d. immobilize the victim, then remove the victim from the water.

53. Emergency care for a snakebite includes:
   a. cleaning the bite with soap and water.
   b. placing ice on the bite.
   c. sucking the venom from the bite.
   d. capturing the snake.

54. Typical signs and symptoms in a heat emergency patient with hot and dry or moist skin include:
   a. heavy perspiration.
   b. little or no perspiration.
   c. muscle cramps.
   d. weak pulse.

55. Typical signs and symptoms in a heat emergency patient with normal or cool moist, pale skin include:
       a. rapid pulse.
       b. seizures.
       c. little or no perspiration.
       d. muscle cramps.

56. An example of a medical condition that can mimic a psychiatric condition is:
       a. heart attack.
       b. diabetes.
       c. asthma.
       d. allergic reaction.

57. Proper treatment of a hostile or aggressive patient includes:
       a. restraining the patient.
       b. encouraging the patient to accept emergency care.
       c. calling a physician.
       d. watching for sudden changes in behavior.

58. Proper restraint of a violent patient includes:
       a. Handcuffs.
       b. Plastic restraints.
       c. Leather cuffs.
       d. "Hog-tying."

59. Proper care for a child with epiglottitis should include:
       a. taking the child's temperature.
       b. putting the child in a supine position.
       c. inserting an oral airway.
       d. transporting the child to the hospital.

60. In treating an infant or child with fever, you should:
       a. apply rubbing alcohol to reduce the patient's temperature.
       b. transport the patient to the hospital.
       c. submerge the child in cold water.
       d. apply towels soaked in cold water.

Questions 61 to 63 pertain to the following scenario:
       The mother of a 4-year-old boy calls you because her son is "unning a high fever. The boy has been vomiting and has diarrhea. His temperature is 103ºF.

61. The best line of treatment for a child with diarrhea and vomiting is to
       a. allow the child to sip some water or chipped ice.
       b. maintain an open airway and administer oxygen.
       c. insert an oropharyngeal airway.
       d. administer an antidiarrheal.

62. To first step in assessing a child with fever should be to:
       a. obtain an oral temperature.
       b. obtain a rectal temperature.
       c. determine the child's temperature using a skin thermometer.
       d. cover the child with towels soaked in tepid water.

63. On transport to the hospital, the child suddenly has a seizure. You should immediately:
    a. provide oxygen.
    b. insert an oropharyngeal airway.
    c. insert a bite stick.
    d. keep the child covered and wait until arrival at the hospital.

64. Signs of iron poisoning in a child include:
    a. hyperventilation.
    b. drowsiness.
    c. irritability.
    d. bloody vomiting.

65. In treating a child with meningitis, an EMT-B should always:
    a. assess for shock.
    b. call medical direction.
    c. wear a surgical mask.
    d. obtain a relative skin temperature.

66. Which of the following statements regarding use of the ambulance siren is FALSE?
    a. Use the siren when close to alert the driver of a vehicle ahead.
    b. Continuous use of a siren can increase an operator's driving speed.
    c. Use of a siren can make motorists less inclined to give the right of way.
    d. Use of a siren can worsen the condition of a patient.

67. En route to a call, an emergency vehicle is **NOT** allowed to:
    a. pass in a no-passing zone.
    b. exceed the speed limit.
    c. pass a school bus with red lights blinking.
    d. pass through a stop sign.

68. Which of the following statements regarding use of visual warning devices in an emergency vehicle is FALSE?
    a. Headlights should be kept on both day and night.
    b. Four-way flashers can be used as emergency lights.
    c. Alternating flashing headlights should only be used if attached to secondary head lamps.
    d. Lights should blink in tandem rather than in an alternating pattern.

69. Which of the following steps should be taken when transporting a patient to the hospital?
    a. More time should be spent packaging a highly traumatized patient.
    b. Sheets and blankets should be kept as loose as possible.
    c. Trauma patients should be secured to a spine board or other carrying device.
    d. A highly traumatized patient should not be moved until emergency treatment is completed.

70. Vital signs should be assessed:
    a. every 15 minutes in an unstable patient.
    b. every 5 minutes in an unstable patient.
    c. every 10 minutes in a stable patient.
    d. every 10 minutes in an unstable patient.

71. When transferring a patient without serious injury to the emergency department, you should:
    a. keep the patient in the ambulance until the operator decides where he or she should be taken.
    b. bring the patient directly into the emergency room, then leave the scene.
    c. place the patient in a hospital bed, then leave the scene.
    d. submit a prehospital care report, then leave the scene.

72. Which of the following statements regarding stabilization of a collision vehicle is TRUE?
    a. A vehicle upright on four wheels should be considered stable.
    b. The tires on an upright vehicle should be deflated.
    c. To stabilize a vehicle that has fallen on its side, kneel down to place cribbing.
    d. Stabilization is required in a vehicle with a crushed roof.

73. In the care of a patient with hazardous materials injuries, you should:
    a. make sure the patient has been decontaminated.
    b. transport the patient immediately.
    c. begin care only after the patient has been moved to a safe zone.
    d. wait for arrival of the hazardous materials (hazmat) team before treating the patient.

74. In initial triage, a patient in cardiac arrest is considered Priority 1 in the following situation:
    a. under all circumstances.
    b. in cases of severe hypothermia.
    c. in cases of cold water drowning.
    d. when ample resources are available.

75. In the case of a multiple-casualty incident, patients should be transported:
    a. immediately.
    b. only under the direction of a transportation officer.
    c. within 30 minutes of notification.
    d. under direction of radio dispatch.

76. A child's airway differs from that of an adult because:
    a. the tongue is smaller.
    b. the chest wall is more rigid.
    c. the tongue is larger.
    d. the trachea is wider.

77. Signs of inadequate breathing in both adults and children include:
    a. seesaw breathing.
    b. cyanosis.
    c. diminished breath sounds.
    d. inability to speak.

78. Which of the following is **NOT** a complication of orotracheal intubation?
    a. Hypoxia
    b. Soft-tissue trauma
    c. Increased heart rate
    d. Decreased heart rate

79. What is the problem in the case of an infiltrated IV?
    a. the IV fluid flows into surrounding tissue.
    b. the IV flow rate is too fast.
    c. tubing is caught under the backboard.
    d. tubing has pulled out of the catheter.

80. A potentially serious sign or symptom associated with an acute stress reaction is:
    a. difficulty sleeping.
    b. nausea.
    c. loss of appetite.
    d. uncontrollable crying.

Questions 81 to 83 pertain to the following scenario:
    You are called to the scene of a car accident involving a 30-year-old woman and her 3-year-old son. The brakes on the car failed, causing the woman to hit a tree. Both the mother and her son have lost consciousness.

81. The first step in assessing the mother should be:
    a. perform CPR.
    b. determine responsiveness.
    c. open the airway.
    d. resuscitate for 1 minute, then activate EMS.

82. The first step in assessing the child should be:
    a. resuscitate for 1 minute, then activate EMS.
    b. open the airway.
    c. activate EMS.
    d. take a pulse.

83. To assess circulation in the child, you should:
    a. feel for the brachial artery.
    b. feel for the carotid artery.
    c. perform chest compression.
    d. perform CPR.

84. If an adult patient has stopped breathing but has a pulse, you should:
    a. perform chest compression.
    b. begin CPR.
    c. provide rescue breathing.
    d. open the airway.

85. To open the airway of an unconscious patient with a possible spinal injury:
    a. perform the head-tilt maneuver.
    b. perform the chin-lift maneuver.
    c. rotate the patient's head.
    d. perform the jaw-thrust maneuver.

86. In the case of a patient with gastric distention and vomiting, you should:
    a. turn the patient's head.
    b. roll the patient onto his side.
    c. place the patient in a supine position.
    d. perform rescue breathing.

87. The correct position for releasing chest compression should be to:
    a. place your hands on the patient's sternum and move from the hips.
    b. lift your hands away from the sternum.
    c. bend your elbows and lift your hands from the sternum.
    d. keep your knees and elbows bent.

88. Muscles connect to bones via which of the following:
    a. ligaments.
    b. nerves.
    c. myofibril.
    d. tendons.

89. In treating a laceration, you should:
    a. gently probe the edges of the laceration to see the extent of the wound.
    b. apply butterfly bandages and leave the patient in the emergency department.
    c. check the patient's pulse.
    d. bandage the laceration immediately.

90. In caring for a patient with a puncture wound from an impaled object, you should:
    a. remove the object.
    b. put pressure on the object.
    c. bandage the wounded area.
    d. stabilize the object.

91. The best way to save an avulsed body part is to:
    a. put the part in dry ice.
    b. immerse the part in ice water.
    c. wrap the part in a dry sterile dressing.
    d. immerse the part in saline.

92. Which of the following statements regarding abdominal bullet wounds is **TRUE**?
    a. An abdominal gunshot wound without an exit wound can be dangerous.
    b. Internal abdominal injury from a bullet wound can be easily detected.
    c. Only the area directly underneath an entrance wound may be seriously injured.
    d. Only the area directly underneath an exit wound may be seriously injured.

93. Which of the following statements regarding burns is **FALSE**?
    a. Chemical burns can burn continuously for days.
    b. Alkaline chemicals can enter the bloodstream via burns.
    c. The age of the patient should be considered when assessing burns.
    d. An electrical burn is usually not serious.

94. According to the rule of nines, which of the following is **TRUE?**
    a. an infant's head involves the same amount of body surface as an adult's.
    b. an infant's head accounts for 18% of body surface.
    c. each lower limb in an adult accounts for 13.5% of body surface.
    d. an adult's head accounts for 18% of body surface.

95. Which of the following types of burns can be treated by flushing with water?
    a. carbolic acid
    b. dry lime
    c. hydrofluoric acid
    d. electrical burns

96. Chemical burns to the eyes should be treated by:
    a. flushing with vinegar or baking soda.
    b. covering the eye with a moistened pad.
    c. flooding the eye with water for at least 20 minutes.
    d. covering the eye and transporting the patient.

97. In bandaging an open wound, you should take care to:
   a. cover the fingers and toes.
   b. leave the fingers and toes exposed.
   c. remove blood-soaked dressings.
   d. tightly bandage the wound.

Questions 98 to 100 pertain to the following scenario:
   You are called to the scene of a traffic accident involving a sport utility vehicle (SUV) and a city bus. The elderly driver of the SUV had suffered a heart attack behind the wheel and crashed into the bus. Of the 15 passengers on the bus, 5 have multiple bone injuries, 2 severe head trauma and bleeding, 2 difficulty breathing, 2 back injuries, and 4 musculoskeletal or soft-tissue injuries. The bus driver has a probable spinal cord injury.

98. In initial triage, the 2 patients with breathing difficulties should be classified as:
   a. priority 2.
   b. priority 1.
   c. priority 4.
   d. priority 3.

99. The elderly driver of the SUV has gone into cardiac arrest. This patient should be classified as:
   a. priority 1.
   b. priority 4.
   c. priority 2.
   d. priority 3.

100. The bus driver should be classified as:
   a. priority 1.
   b. priority 4.
   c. priority 2.
   d. priority 3.

101. Which of the following is the correct sequence of connective function?
   a. Muscle-ligament-bone
   b. Bone-muscle-ligament
   c. Muscle-tendon-bone
   d. Muscle-bone-tendon

Questions 102 to 104 pertain to the following scenario:
   During an ice storm, the car of a 25-year-old man skids off the road and crashes into the side of a grocery store. His right arm is bleeding profusely, with the end of the bone protruding through the skin. The patient also reports severe pain in his right femur.

102. The first step in treating this patient is to:
   a. push the protruding bone back into place.
   b. assess for life-threatening injury.
   c. align the bone in a neutral position.
   d. transport to the hospital immediately.

103. The proper care for this patient's protruding bone is to:
   a. realign the injury and splint.
   b. push the bone back into place.
   c. immobilize the patient on a long spine board.
   d. splint the injury in the position in which it was found.

104. The best method of treatment for the patient's injured femur is to:
   a. use a rigid splint.
   b. use a formable splint.
   c. use a traction splint.
   d. immobilize the patient on a long spine board.

105. To treat an open abdominal injury, you should:
   a. apply an occlusive dressing using aluminum foil.
   b. replace any eviscerated or exposed organs.
   c. give the patient sips of water.
   d. apply a sterile saline dressing.

106. Which of the following statements regarding shoulder girdle injuries is **TRUE**?
   a. A dislocated shoulder can sometimes go back into place.
   b. Use a rigid splint for shoulder injuries.
   c. Always attempt to straighten out a dislocated shoulder.
   d. If spinal injury is suspected, tie a sling around the patient's neck.

107. A hip fracture is a fracture of the:
   a. pelvis.
   b. proximal femur.
   c. pubic bone.
   d. humerus bone.

108. In treating an ankle or foot injury, you should:
   a. apply manual traction.
   b. apply an ice pack directly to the skin.
   c. change the position of the ankle.
   d. tie a pillow to the ankle and foot.

109. Use of the PASG is indicated in cases of:
   a. cardiogenic shock.
   b. shock in the presence of a chest wound.
   c. pelvic injury.
   d. congestive heart failure.

110. A blood glucose meter reading of 145 indicates:
   a. hypoglycemia.
   b. hyperglycemia.
   c. diabetes.
   d. normal blood sugar level.

111. Which of the following statements is **FALSE**?
   a. A diabetic adult is at higher risk of a medical emergency than a diabetic child.
   b. Altered mental status may be caused by diabetes.
   c. Meningitis may cause altered mental status.
   d. Altered mental status may be associated with alcohol use.

112. According to the Ryan White act, if an EMT is possibly exposed to a bloodborne disease, which procedure should be followed:
   a. A hospital is required to test the patient for bloodborne diseases if requested.
   b. A hospital is required to review the patient's medical records for evidence of bloodborne disease.
   c. A hospital is required to test the patient if requested by a designated officer.
   d. The patient must be tested for disease within 48 hours.

113. Which of the following statements regarding consent is **FALSE**?
    a. Care may be given to a child without parental consent.
    b. Expressed consent must be given by all patients before treatment is given.
    c. In the case of an unconscious patient, consent may be assumed.
    d. A mentally impaired patient has the right to refuse treatment.

114. According to patient confidentiality requirements:
    a. patient information can be disclosed if the patient grants verbal permission.
    b. patient information cannot be shared with other healthcare personnel.
    c. patient information can only be disclosed if the patient signs a written release.
    d. patient information can be disclosed while calling medical direction.

115. A supine patient is positioned:
    a. on the back.
    b. on the abdomen.
    c. on one side.
    d. seated with legs straight out.

116. In the Trendelenburg position, the patient is in which state:
    a. Lying on one side.
    b. Lying on the abdomen.
    c. Lying with the head lower than the feet.
    d. Leaning back in a semi-seated position.

117. A fractured rib may cause:
    a. shock.
    b. cyanosis.
    c. altered mental status.
    d. inadequate breathing.

118. The preferred method for moving a patient down a set of stairs is to:
    a. carry the patient on your back.
    b. use a stair chair.
    c. carry the patient on a stretcher.
    d. lean forward from your hips.

119. Which of the following may be used to move a patient with suspected spinal injury?
    a. Urgent moves
    b. Extremity lift
    c. Direct carry
    d. Draw-sheet method

120. Which statement regarding the danger zone of an accident scene is **FALSE**?
    a. The danger zone extends at least 50 feet in all directions.
    b. Park the ambulance inside the danger zone to better assist victims.
    c. Park the ambulance away from the poles on which downed wires are attached.
    d. The size of the danger zone depends on the nature and severity of the accident.

121. As a BSI precaution, you should:
    a. determine the mechanism of injury.
    b. assess the crime scene.
    c. wear a protective mask.
    d. assess mental status.

122. A "fender-bender" occurs between two cars in a parking lot. Both drivers claim they are unhurt, although the male driver was thrown against the steering wheel on impact. The best course of action would be to:
    a. assume both drivers have sustained no injuries.
    b. identify the mechanism of injury and treat accordingly.
    c. treat only the driver who was thrown against the wheel.
    d. report the accident and leave the scene.

123. Which of the following does **NOT** indicate a life-threatening condition?
    a. inadequate circulation
    b. heavy bleeding
    c. difficulty breathing
    d. hypoglycemia

124. Typical changes to a woman's body during late pregnancy include:
    a. increased blood pressure.
    b. increased cardiac output.
    c. reduced heart rate.
    d. reduced blood volume.

125. Amniotic fluid is normally:
    a. greenish.
    b. brownish.
    c. clear.
    d. mixed with blood.

126. Which of the following statements regarding the first stage of labor is **FALSE**?
    a. The first stage can last up to 16 hours.
    b. The first stage may last less than 4 hours.
    c. Watery, bloody discharge may occur.
    d. Contractions last 30 seconds to 1 minute.

Questions 127 to 129 pertain to the following scenario:
    You receive a call from a panicked taxicab driver, telling you that a woman is having a baby in his cab. When you arrive, a crowd has gathered around the cab. A woman is lying in the back seat, moaning. She complains of needing to go to the bathroom.

127. The first step in caring for this patient is to
    a. allow her to go to the bathroom.
    b. tell bystanders to leave.
    c. transport the patient to the hospital.
    d. remove the patient's clothing to view the vaginal opening.

128. Bulging is visible at the vaginal opening. The patient insists that she does not want to have the baby in the cab and begs you to take her to the hospital. You should:
    a. transport the patient to the hospital.
    b. elevate the patient's buttocks with blankets or a pillow and prepare for delivery.
    c. prepare for delivery by positioning the patient with one foot on the car seat and one on the floor.
    d. time the patient's contractions.

129. In delivering the baby, you should
    a. place one hand below the baby's head.
    b. gently pull on the baby to facilitate delivery.
    c. once the head delivers, tell the mother to push.
    d. gently grasp the baby by the feet.

130. To establish that a baby is breathing, you should:
   a. hold the baby up by the feet and slap the buttocks.
   b. snap your index finger against the sole of the foot.
   c. provide supplemental oxygen by placing tubing in the baby's mouth.
   d. suction the baby's nose.

131. In delivering the placenta, you should:
   a. put pressure on the mother's abdomen over the uterus.
   b. leave afterbirth tissue within the uterus.
   c. save the afterbirth in a container.
   d. check for meconium staining.

Questions 132 to 134 pertain to the following scenario:
   The sister of an 80-year-old man reports that her brother is bleeding profusely. On arrival, the man is conscious and lying on the couch with his legs up. The seat of his pants is soaked in blood, as are the towels placed underneath. The patient states that he is bleeding from his rectum. The bleeding began after dinner, when he felt a sharp pain in his lower abdomen.

132. Severe blood loss in an adult is defined as:
   a. 150 cc
   b. 250 cc
   c. 500 cc
   d. 1000 cc

133. To estimate the amount of blood lost, you should:
   a. pour a pint of fluid on the floor and soak a garment in it.
   b. wait for signs of hypoperfusion to appear.
   c. remove the patient's clothing.
   d. ask the patient.

134. The first line of treatment for this patient would be to:
   a. ensure an open airway.
   b. obtain a detailed history.
   c. wait for signs of hypoperfusion to appear.
   d. administer CPR.

135. A tourniquet should be used:
   a. to control external bleeding from an extremity.
   b. for joint injuries.
   c. as a last resort.
   d. to control internal bleeding from an extremity.

136. A large piece of glass becomes lodged in the eye of a bystander during a bar fight. The best line of treatment should be to:
   a. attempt to remove the piece of glass.
   b. place a paper cup over the piece of glass.
   c. assess for signs of shock.
   d. apply a bandage over the piece of glass.

137. Which of the following statements regarding a twin birth is **FALSE**?
   a. There may be a separate placenta for each baby.
   b. The second baby may deliver in a breech position.
   c. The placenta delivers only after the second twin is born.
   d. The umbilical cord of the first twin should be cut before the second twin is born.

138. In treating a woman who has miscarried, you should:
   a. save all expelled tissues.
   b. pack the vagina to absorb bleeding.
   c. replace expelled tissues in the vagina.
   d. discard any blood-soaked pads.

139. Which of the following statements regarding intubation is **FALSE**?
   a. Press on the throat to push the vocal cords into view.
   b. Air sounds should be heard in the epigastrium.
   c. Hold the tube against the patient's teeth to prevent it from moving.
   d. You may only need one hand to work the BVM.

140. Activated charcoal may be safely used in:
   a. patients with altered mental status.
   b. patients who have ingested acid.
   c. patients who have ingested gasoline.
   d. patients who have ingested aspirin.

141. The first course of treatment for a poisoning victim is:
   a. syrup of ipecac.
   b. activated charcoal.
   c. sorbitol.
   d. antidote.

Questions 142 to 144 pertain to the following scenario:
   You are called to the scene of an outdoor festival by the sister of a young woman who has been stung by a bee. The patient is sitting on the ground and is breathing rapidly. She reports nausea and her skin is flushed and blotchy. Hives are visible in the area around the sting. The patient's sister says she had an allergic reaction to a bee sting as a child.

142. The first step in treating this patient would be to:
   a. administer epinephrine.
   b. begin care for shock.
   c. administer oxygen.
   d. request an ALS intercept.

143. The patient is unable to get up and appears disoriented. She has a rapid pulse and her blood pressure is low. You should proceed by:
   a. treating for shock.
   b. administering epinephrine.
   c. administering oxygen.
   d. calling medical direction.

144. The patient's sister suddenly remembers that her sister had been prescribed epinephrine for the allergic reaction she experienced as a child. In this case, you should:
   a. treat for shock.
   b. consult medical direction and administer epinephrine.
   c. provide artificial ventilation and transport.
   d. monitor vital signs and transport.

Questions 145 to 147 pertain to the following scenario:
On a busy city street, a 50-year-old woman has been knocked down by a bike messenger. She is conscious and sitting on the step of a building. The patient says she automatically extended her right hand to break the fall. Her right wrist is bruised and swollen and her right knee joint is locked into an abnormal position. She complains of feeling "pins and needles" in her right hand.

145. The first step in treating this patient's injuries is to:
    a. assess distal PMS.
    b. splint.
    c. realign the wrist.
    d. apply a cervical collar.

146. In treating the patient's wrist injury, you should:
    a. induce crepitus.
    b. realign the wrist.
    c. splint.
    d. apply wet heat.

147. In treating the patient's knee injury, you should:
    a. splint in the found position.
    b. realign.
    c. apply an ice pack.
    d. apply wet heat.

148. Proper care of an injury to the fibula or tibia includes:
    a. treating for shock.
    b. applying an ice pack.
    c. applying wet heat.
    d. applying manual traction.

149. Which of the following statements regarding concussion is **FALSE**?
    a. Concussion usually causes no detectable brain damage.
    b. Concussion may be associated with amnesia.
    c. Concussion may result in long-term memory loss.
    d. Concussion may or may not result in loss of consciousness.

150. In removing a child from a car safety seat, you should:
    a. slide the child out of the seat.
    b. strap the child across the abdomen.
    c. tape the child across the chin.
    d. apply a cervical collar.

Answers and Explanations

1. B: The first step in treating a patient with potential cardiac arrest is to administer oxygen. At that point, you should obtain a patient history and perform a physical exam to obtain baseline vital signs.

2. D: When a patient loses consciousness, the first step is to open the airway. If you find the patient to be in cardiac arrest based on your initial assessment, you should attach an automated external defibrillator.

3. B. In addition to administering oxygen, the most effective way to decrease oxygen demand is to calm and reassure the patient. Driving at high speed, flashing lights, or turning on the siren will only heighten the patient's distress.

4. C: In a young child with possible airway obstruction, attempts to remove a mild obstruction may result in severe obstruction. Back blows and chest thrusts should only be performed in the case of a severe obstruction, and finger sweeps only when the child is unconscious and the object is visible in the mouth. The most appropriate course of action is to avoid agitating the child and provide immediate transport to the hospital.

5. A: Young children typically fear a stranger in their environment and will maintain eye contact with that person. Thus, inattentiveness to your presence is indicative of an altered mental state.

6. D: High fever, generalized rash, and altered mental state are indicative of meningitis, or inflammation of the tissue protecting the brain and spinal cord. Because a child with meningitis is at high risk for seizures, his or her condition should be carefully monitored during transport to the hospital.

7.C: Rapid trauma assessment is indicated in patients with significant mechanisms of injury, such as penetrating wounds to the head, neck, chest, or abdomen, falls from a height of >15 feet (such as from a tall building), or multiple long bone fractures.

8. D: In patients with acute ischemic stroke, administering oxygen is the most important first step, followed by rapid transport to the hospital for fibrinolytic therapy. Fibrinolytic therapy must be performed within 3 hours of symptom onset.

9. C: Crowning indicates that the second stage of labor has begun and delivery is imminent. After stopping the ambulance, gentle pressure should be applied to the infant's head to avoid explosive delivery.

10. B: If the umbilical cord continues to pulsate and the infant is not breathing adequately, the cord should remain attached and the head of the infant kept at the level of the mother's perineum until arrival at the hospital. The umbilical cord should not be clamped or cut until the cord has stopped pulsating and the infant has begun to breathe normally.

11. B: It may be difficult to extend the head and flex the neck of an elderly person because of arthritic conditions. The head of an elderly person should never be forced back. Rather, the jaw should be thrust forward and the tongue pulled out of the airway.

12. A: Two major risk factors for airway obstruction in elderly patients are poorly chewed food and dentures. If dentures are loose or ill-fitting and/or obstruct efforts to ventilate the patient, they should be removed.

13. C: When a patient begins to make gurgling sounds, whether before, during, or after ventilation, he or she should be suctioned immediately; however, a patient should be properly oxygenated before suctioning.

14. C: An EMT-B can help prevent future falls in an elderly patient by assessing the patient's home for potential hazards, such as slippery rugs or obstructive furniture.

15. D: Oral glucose, activated charcoal, and oxygen are carried on an ambulance and may be administered to a patient under certain circumstances.

16. A: If previously prescribed for the patient, the EMT-B may assist him or her in taking nitroglycerin, epinephrine, or inhalers. Permission from medical direction may be required.

17. B: Blood loss, trauma, particularly from abdominal injury, infection, and dehydration resulting from diarrhea or vomiting are the most common causes of hypoperfusion in infants and children. Bleeding that may not seem serious in an adult may lead to hypoperfusion in a child.

18. C: Signs of hypoperfusion in a child include rapid respiratory rate, pale, clammy skin, weak or absent peripheral pulse, and decreased urinary output.

19. D: Because infants and children may go into decompensated shock rapidly, never wait for signs of decompensated shock to develop. Supplemental oxygen should be provided, external bleeding managed, and artificial ventilation begun if necessary. The child should be kept warm and transported immediately to the hospital.

20. A: Although a cardiac condition is the most likely cause of cardiac arrest in adults, respiratory failure is the most likely cause in children. Breathing difficulties in children may result from airway obstruction or respiratory disease.

21. C: Because the patient has been lying in the cold all night, he is most likely suffering from hypothermia. Signs of hypothermia include muscular rigidity, amnesia, and loss of contact with environment.

22. D: The best course of action to prevent additional body heat loss in an injured patient trapped in cold environment is to create a barrier to the cold. Blankets or articles of clothing can be used to protect the patient from exposure to wind or water. Active rewarming may result in cardiac arrest, and ingestion of stimulants in impaired circulation.

23. A: Individuals under the influence of alcohol or drugs may be more susceptible to hypothermia. The fact that the patient had been drinking and was trapped overnight in a cold environment places him at high risk of hypothermia.

24. B: The signs and symptoms of carbon monoxide poisoning may resemble those of the flu, including nausea and headache.

25. A: The first step in treating a patient with an absorbed poison is to remove the poison from the eyes or skin immediately. This may be accomplished by irrigating the eye or skin with clean water for 20 minutes. Attempting to neutralize the absorbed substance with other solutions such as vinegar or baking soda may make the injury worse.

26. B: Other conditions such as diabetes, epilepsy, and hypoxia may produce symptoms resembling those of alcohol intoxication. Given that the patient has hit his head, his symptoms could be due to head injury.

27. A: Because intoxicated patients could also be suffering from a medical emergency or an injury, they should be transported to the hospital for further assessment. Patients with even minor head injuries may be prone to subdural hematoma. Asking the patient if he has taken drugs may provoke a violent reaction; however, calling law enforcement without properly assessing the patient's condition may result in serious adverse events or even death.

28. C: Substance or alcohol abusers may appear calm and then suddenly become violent. For your own protection, if the situation becomes unsafe and you have not been trained in law enforcement, you should immediately leave the scene and call the police for assistance.

29. D: Breath sounds should always be heard bilaterally. If breath sounds are absent on the left but present on the right, the endotracheal tube has been incorrectly inserted into the right bronchus. If breath sounds are only present in the epigastrium, the esophagus has been intubated, which may result in a life-threatening condition.

30. D: The accuracy of an oximeter reading may be affected in patients in shock or with hypothermia because low body temperature restricts blood flow through the capillaries. Carbon monoxide poisoning produces falsely high readings; because cigarettes produce carbon monoxide, chronic smokers may also have falsely high readings.

31. A: SAMPLE stands for the elements of a patient's history, including signs and symptoms, past medical history, and use of medications. It is always important to obtain a patient's medication history, especially in the case of an older patient.

32. B: Sweating is an example of a vital sign. Taking a patient's vital signs and symptoms is the first step in obtaining a SAMPLE history.

33. C: Nitroglycerin is usually prescribed for patients with angina pectoris, or chest pain.

34. D: Compared with adults, infants and children have a faster pulse and respiratory rate and lower blood pressure.

35. C: Oral requests from a family member are not sufficient reason to withhold care. If a legal DNR (Do Not Resuscitate) order is not presented, an EMT-B is obligated to provide care.

36. B: In some states, an off-duty EMT-B has no legal obligation to provide care; however, you may feel a moral obligation to help a patient in need. It is always best to provide care and contact other emergency personnel for additional help. Leaving the scene of an accident, even after providing care, may be construed as abandoning a patient.

37. C: Mental status, condition of the airway, breathing, and circulation should be assessed in all patients, whether responsive or unresponsive, and with either trauma or a medical condition. Capillary refill is used to assess infants and children only.

38. B: The normal pulse rate for an adult is between 60 and 100 beats per minute. In an emergency situation, the pulse rate may rise to between 100 and 140 beats per minute. A pulse rate below 50 beats per minute indicates a serious problem.

39. D: A high pulse in a child is usually not a cause for concern; however, a low pulse may be indicative of imminent cardiac arrest.

40. C: Because your thumb has its own pulse, you should not use it to take someone else's pulse. Applying too much pressure can press the artery shut. The carotid pulse should not be assessed on both sides at the same time; rather, if you have difficulty finding a pulse on one side, try the other side.

41. B: Soft-tissue trauma to the head, face, or neck is indicative of cervical spine injury.

42. A: In the case of a potential cervical spine injury, you should immediately stabilize the patient's head and neck manually. The head and neck should be stabilized until he or she is completely immobilized and secured to a backboard.

43. B: In the case of possible cervical spine injury, a rigid collar should be applied before transporting the patient to the hospital; a soft collar is not sufficient to immobilize the cervical spine. The patient's head should be kept in a neutral position, not turned to one side or tilted front or back. Once the collar is in place, the back of the neck cannot be palpated.

44. C: A detailed physical exam is most often performed on a trauma patient with a significant mechanism of injury rather than a patient with no significant injury or a medical patient.

45. D: Oxygen should never be withheld from a patient in respiratory distress, even those with a chronic lung disease such as bronchitis or emphysema.

46. C: Gurgling sounds usually indicate the presence of fluid in the throat.

47. B: COPD patients with difficulty breathing are typically in the tripod position, leaning forward with hands on knees.

48. C: Altered mental status in a patient with breathing difficulty usually indicates a lack of oxygen. If the patient is not breathing adequately, artificial ventilation should be performed and supplemental oxygen should be provided.

49. D: Never rub or squeeze a frostbitten or frozen area, as this can seriously damage the injured tissue. Active rewarming is seldom recommended in cases of frostbite or freezing because of the risk of permanent injury. You should administer high-concentration oxygen, cover the frozen or frostbitten area, and transport the patient to the hospital immediately.

50. B: If transport is delayed and the local protocol recommends it, begin active rewarming of the frozen area, taking care that the injured area does not touch the sides or bottom of the container. Never massage or rub snow on a frostbitten or frozen area. Patients should not be allowed to smoke or drink alcoholic beverages because of the risk of decreasing circulation.

51. C: During the course of active rewarming, keep the affected area immersed until the water cools, even if the patient complains of pain, then remove the affected part and add more warm water; complaints of moderate or even intense pain indicate that rewarming has been successful. Do not apply pressure or allow the patient to walk on the affected area. Once rewarming has been completed, apply a dry sterile dressing to the affected area and cover with blankets, but do not allow the blanket to come into contact with the injured area.

52. B: In the case of a near-drowning, rescue breathing should be initiated without delay, even if the victim is still in the water. Chest compression is only effective when the victim is out of the water.

53. A: Never attempt to suck the venom from a snakebite. Do not put ice on the bite unless instructed to do so by a physician or local protocol. The bite should be cleaned with soap and water and the patient transported to the hospital immediately.

54. B: Typical signs and symptoms in a heat emergency patient with hot and dry or moist skin include little or no perspiration, full and rapid pulse, and seizures but not muscle cramps.

55. D: Typical signs and symptoms of a heat emergency patient with normal or cool moist, pale skin include muscle cramps, heavy perspiration, and weak pulse rate.

56. B: Diabetes or low blood sugar can produce symptoms--such as hostile behavior, drooling, heavy perspiration, or seizures--that mimic those of a psychiatric condition.

57. D: The best approach in treating a hostile or aggressive patient is to watch for sudden changes in behavior and seek assistance from law enforcement. Restraining the patient or forcing him or her to accept emergency care is usually not in the legal jurisdiction of an EMT-B.

58. C: Soft restraints such as leather cuffs or belts are acceptable means of restraint for violent patients; handcuffs or plastic "throwaway" restraints may cause soft tissue damage. "Hog-tying" can impair breathing and result in positional asphyxia.

59. D: Never place an object such as a thermometer, tongue blade, or oral airway into the mouth of a child with epiglottitis, as this could obstruct the airway. The child should not be forced to lie down, which may be uncomfortable, but should be transported to the hospital in a sitting position on his or her parent's lap.

60. B: Do not use rubbing alcohol to reduce the child's temperature, because it can be toxic if absorbed in high amounts. Submerging the child in cold water or applying cold towels can result in hypothermia. The child should be transported to the hospital as soon as possible.

61. B: The best line of treatment for a child with diarrhea and vomiting is to maintain an open airway and administer oxygen. Oral suctioning may be required for vomiting. Sipping water or ice chips is usually recommended for children with diarrhea only.

62. C: The first step in assessing a child with fever is to obtain a relative skin temperature using a skin thermometer or by applying the back of your hand to the child's forehead or abdomen. Oral or rectal temperatures are generally not taken in the prehospital setting.

63. A: If a child has a seizure on transport, you should maintain an open airway and administer oxygen. Never insert an oropharyngeal airway or a bite stick. Seizures caused by fever should always be considered life-threatening.

64. D: Consuming even small amounts of iron can be life-threatening in children. Usual signs of iron poisoning include nausea, diarrhea, and bloody vomiting.

65. C: Because meningitis is an airborne disease, a surgical mask should always be worn when caring for a child with suspected meningitis. An EMT-B with possible exposure to meningitis should be evaluated by a physician as soon as possible.

66. A: Sounding the siren when close to another vehicle can result in the driver panicking and jamming on his brakes; use the horn to alert the driver instead. Continuous use of a siren can make motorists less likely to yield the right of way, can increase stress and anxiety in injured or ill patients, and has been associated with increased operator driving speed.

67. C: An emergency vehicle is allowed to pass in a no-passing zone, exceed the speed limit, and pass through a stop sign as long as it is safe to do so; however, in the case of a school bus with blinking red lights, the operator of the vehicle should wait for the bus driver to clear the children and turn off the red lights.

68. B: Four-way flashers or directional signals should not be used as emergency lights because they can confuse other drivers.

69. C: Highly traumatized patients should be transported to the hospital as soon as possible; spending too much time packaging a patient in this condition can result in death. In some cases, the patient must be moved before emergency care is completed. Sheets and blankets should be tucked under the mattress and stretcher and the patient secured to a spine board or other patient-carrying device.

70. B: Vital signs should be assessed every 5 minutes in an unstable patient and every 15 minutes in a stable patient.

71. A: A non-emergency patient should never be left alone; an EMT-B should remain with the patient at all times. In cases when the emergency department is especially busy, the patient can remain in the ambulance until the operator decides where he or she should be taken.

72. B: Although a vehicle that is upright on all four wheels appears stable, it can be rocked forward or backward or side to side, possibly injuring those inside; the tires of an upright vehicle should always be deflated during stabilization. When placing cribbing, you should never kneel down; maintain a squatting position on both feet to move quickly in case the car moves suddenly. Stabilization is unnecessary only in the case of a car with its roof crushed flat against the body.

73. A: Always make sure the patient has been decontaminated before transporting him or her to the hospital; a contaminated patient or EMT-B can contaminate the entire ambulance team. If a patient requires immediate life-saving care, even if he or she has not been decontaminated, you should provide that care, being careful to wear protective clothing and to decontaminate yourself as soon as possible.

74. D: A patient in cardiac arrest is considered Priority 4 or 0 because immediate treatment in such a patient is not justified when many other individuals need attention; however, such patients can be upgraded to Priority 1 when ample resources become available.

75. B. In the case of an accident involving multiple casualties, an ambulance should not transport patients without approval of the transportation officer; failure to comply with the directions of a transportation officer could result in patients being taken to the wrong treatment facility.

76. C: In a child, the tongue is larger, the chest wall is softer, and the trachea is narrower compared with those of an adult.

77. A: Seesaw breathing, in which the chest and abdomen move in opposite directions, often occurs in children but not adults with inadequate breathing.

78. C: Orotracheal intubation may stimulate the airway, resulting in slowing of the heart rate.

79. A: In the case of an infiltrated IV, the needle has either punctured the vein and exited the other side or pulled out of the vein entirely, resulting in fluid flowing into the surrounding tissue. The IV flow should be stopped and the IV discontinued.

80. D: Signs or symptoms indicative of an acute psychological problem following a stressful event include uncontrollable crying, inappropriate behavior, or irrational thoughts; however, nausea, loss of appetite, or difficulty sleeping are typical reactions and usually do not require intervention.

81. B: The first step in assessing an adult patient who has collapsed is to determine responsiveness. This can be done by gently tapping the patient and asking, "Are you OK?" If the patient is able to respond, resuscitation is unnecessary.

82. A: The first step in treating an unconscious child or infant is to resuscitate for 1 minute, then activate EMS.

83. B: To determine the pulse of an adult or a child, you should feel for the carotid artery; feel for the brachial artery in infants.

84. C: If the patient has a pulse, chest compression is not required. If the patient is not breathing, provide artificial ventilation; if the patient has stopped breathing and has no pulse, begin CPR.

85. D: The jaw-thrust maneuver is the only recommended procedure for opening the airway in an unconscious patient with a possible spinal injury.

86. B: Rescue breathing can blow air into the patient's stomach, causing distention. In the case of gastric distention and vomiting, roll the patient onto his or her side. Simply turning the patient's head can lead to aspiration of vomitus or aggravation of spinal injury.

87. A: When releasing chest compression, you should straighten your arms, lock your elbows, and keep your hands on the patient's sternum. Move from the hips, which should act as a fulcrum.

88. D: Tendons connect muscles to bones.

89. C: A laceration may not seem to be serious, but can result in severe infection or scarring if not treated properly. The patient's pulse should be checked, as well as motor and sensory function distal to the injury.

90. D: Never try to remove an impaled object; twisting or putting pressure on the object can cause additional injury. Instead, stabilize the object by applying a bulky dressing.

91. C: The avulsed body part should be saved by wrapping it in a dry sterile dressing and then placing it in a plastic bag, plastic wrap, or aluminum foil. Do not place the part in dry ice, water, or saline.

92. A: Contrary to popular belief, a gunshot wound to the abdomen without an exit wound may still cause serious injury. Bullets can be deflected or explode, sending out pieces that can injure adjacent areas of the body.

93. D: Although burns caused by electrical current may result in relatively minor skin injury, they can present a high risk of severe internal injury.

94. B: Compared with that of an adult, an infant's head is larger in proportion to the rest of the body; thus, while an adult's head accounts for 9% of body surface area, an infant's head accounts for 18%.

95. C: Burns caused by hydrofluoric acid, a chemical commonly used in manufacturing, should be flushed with water as soon as possible.

96. C: In treating a chemical burn to the eye, immediately flood the eye with water; continue washing the eye during transport for at least 20 minutes or until arrival at the hospital. Do not use vinegar or baking soda to neutralize the chemical.

97. B: In bandaging an open wound, take care not to bandage too tightly or too loosely and do not leave loose ends. Fingers and toes should remain exposed to observe changes in circulation unless they have been burned; in that case, they should be covered.

98. B: Patients with treatable injuries that may be life-threatening such as airway or breathing difficulties should be classified as Priority 1 and treated first.

99. B: A patient who has gone into cardiac arrest should be classified as Priority 4 or 0; these patients should not receive treatment unless none of the other patients are at risk of dying or sustaining long-term disability if left untreated.

100. C: Patients with back injuries with or without spinal cord damage should be classified as Priority 2.

101. C: The correct sequence of connective function is muscle-tendon-bone and bone-ligament-bone.

102. B: A dramatic injury to the extremity such as a protruding bone should not distract you from assessing an accident victim for life-threatening injury, such as a spinal fracture. Multiple fractures, particularly to the femur, can result in life-threatening external or internal bleeding.

103. A: In the case of a deformity such as a protruding bone, you should realign the injury to its correct anatomical position and splint; splinting the deformed part in its original position may worsen the injury.

104. C: Femur fractures often cause spasm of the large muscle groups of the thigh, resulting in severe pain and further soft-tissue injury; for this reason, a traction splint should be used to counteract muscle spasm and reduce pain.

105. D: The best method of care for an open abdominal injury is to apply a sterile saline dressing over the wound, then apply an occlusive dressing. Never give the patient something by mouth or touch or replace an exposed or eviscerated organ; use of an aluminum foil occlusive dressing may cut an eviscerated organ.

106. A: Sometimes a dislocated shoulder will go back into place on its own; never attempt to straighten out a dislocation. A rigid splint should not be used for shoulder injuries. In the case of a possible cervical spine injury, do not tie a sling around the patient's neck.

107. B: A hip fracture is a fracture of the proximal femur, not the pelvis.

108. D: In treating an ankle or foot injury, stabilize the limb, taking care not to change the position of the ankle, and tie a pillow to the ankle and foot. Do not apply manual traction or put an ice pack directly on the skin.

109. C: The pneumatic anti-shock garment (PASG) is indicated in cases of bleeding, pelvic injury, or abdominal trauma; it is contraindicated in patients with cardiogenic shock or shock in the presence of a chest wound.

110. B: A blood glucose meter reading above 120 or 140, depending on the manufacturer, indicates hyperglycemia; a reading below 80 indicates hypoglycemia.

111. A: Diabetic children are at increased risk of a medical emergency compared with diabetic adults.

112. B: Under the Ryan White act, in the case of possible exposure of an EMT to the bodily fluids of a patient with possible bloodborne disease, a hospital is only required to review the patient's medical records for evidence of bloodborne disease. Hospitals cannot test a patient for bloodborne disease simply at the request of an EMT or designated officer.

113. D: Children or mentally incompetent adults cannot legally refuse treatment; however, care can be given to a child without parental consent in the case of life-threatening illness or injury when the parent or guardian is not present.

114. C: Patient information cannot be disclosed based on verbal permission or over the telephone but only if the patient has signed a written release; however, patient information can be discussed with healthcare personnel caring for the patient, such as a doctor or nurse.

115. A: A supine patient is lying on his or her back; a prone patient is lying on his or her abdomen, and a patient lying on his or her side is in the recovery position.

116. C: In the Trendelenburg position, the patient lies with the head slightly lower than the feet; this position is often used to treat patients in shock.

117. D: A fractured rib can cause inadequate breathing and thus be life-threatening.

118. B: The preferred method for moving a patient down stairs is to use a stair chair or wheeled stretcher; this method is usually safer and more efficient.

119. A: When immediate care is necessary, urgent moves may be used to move a patient with spinal injury; however, precautions must be made to avoid further spinal injury. The extremity lift, direct carry, and draw-sheet methods are only used to move patients with no suspected spinal injury.

120. B: Never park the ambulance in the danger zone; the ambulance should be parked away from broken glass or other debris.

121. C: As part of the initial assessment of an accident or crime scene, you should take the necessary body substance isolation (BSI) precautions to avoid exposure to the patient's blood, saliva, and other body fluids. BSI precautions include wearing gloves, protective eyewear, and/or a protective mask when providing patient care.

122. B: In the case of an accident, no matter how minor, always identify the mechanism of injury, determine what injuries are possible, and treat the patient accordingly. Never assume that there are no injuries, even if the patient claims he or she is unhurt. In the case of the driver who was thrown against the wheel, although no signs of bruising or other injury are apparent, he may have sustained blunt-force trauma and should be treated accordingly.

123. D: Inadequate circulation, blood loss, and difficulty breathing are all signs of a life-threatening condition.

124. B: Typical body changes during the last trimester include increases in heart rate, blood volume, and cardiac output; blood pressure usually decreases slightly.

125. C: Normally, amniotic fluid is clear; a greenish or brownish color may indicate maternal or fetal distress. Bleeding does not accompany breakage of the amniotic sac.

126. D: The first stage of labor can be as long as 16 hours or as short as 4 hours and is usually associated with watery, bloody discharge. Contractions lasting 30 seconds to 1 minute indicate that delivery is imminent.

127. B: Your first step is to protect the patient from staring bystanders, asking them to leave in a polite but firm manner. Next, you should help the patient to remove any clothing that obstructs your view of the vaginal opening. A feeling of an impending bowel movement and bulging at the vaginal opening indicate that birth is imminent; however, the patient should not be allowed to use the bathroom. Because the baby may be born any minute, transport is not practical at this time.

128. C: Visible bulging at the vaginal opening indicates that crowning is taking place and that birth is imminent. At this point, it is not practical to transport the patient; instead, you should gently position the mother in the cab with one foot resting on the seat and the other on the floor and prepare for delivery.

129. A: The baby should be supported throughout the entire birth process. Place one hand below the baby's head as it delivers. Tell the mother not to push while you check to make sure the umbilical cord is not wrapped around the baby's neck. Never pull on the baby during delivery; grasping a slippery baby by the feet may cause you to drop the child.

130. B: Assess breathing by snapping your index finger against the sole of the baby's foot. Contrary to popular belief, you should not hold the baby by the feet and slap the buttocks. If supplemental oxygen is needed, place tubing close to but not into the baby's mouth. Suction the baby's mouth first to prevent aspiration of blood, fluids, or other materials into the lungs.

131. C: In delivering the placenta or afterbirth, remember that the process can take 20 to 30 minutes. Do not place pressure on the mother's abdomen. Once the placenta delivers, do not leave any afterbirth tissues in the vagina because of the risk of infection; save the afterbirth in a container and give it to the attending physician on arrival at the hospital.

132. D: In an adult, sudden blood loss of 1000 cc or 1 liter is considered serious; however, because children have a lower blood volume compared with adults, blood loss of 500 cc is considered serious in a child. Blood loss of 150 cc would be serious in an infant.

133. A: Although it is difficult to estimate blood loss, a useful method is to pour a pint of liquid on the floor and soak a garment in it to observe how wet it looks and feels. In a patient with blood loss, do not wait for signs of hypoperfusion or shock to develop to begin treatment.

134. A: In this case, bleeding from the rectum is a sign of internal bleeding, which may rapidly lead to hypoperfusion or shock. In cases of suspected internal bleeding, the first step should be to ensure an open airway and assess breathing and circulation. Do not wait for signs of shock to appear before beginning treatment.

135. C: A tourniquet may cause serious injury to the nerves, muscles, or blood vessels and may result in loss of a limb; for this reason, it should only be used as a last resort in cases of life-threatening bleeding.

136. B: The best line of treatment for an object impaled in the eye such as a piece of glass is to place a roll of 3-inch gauze bandage on each side of the object to stabilize it, then place a paper cup over the object and allow it to rest on the rolls of gauze. Do not place a bandage directly over the object or the cup.

137. C: In a twin birth, the placenta may deliver either before or after the birth of the second twin. There may be a separate placenta for each baby or a single one for both. Breech birth is common in the second twin; the umbilical cord of the first twin should be tied or cut before the birth of the second twin.

138. A: In the case of a miscarriage, always save the expelled tissues but do not attempt to replace or remove them from the vagina. Blood-soaked pads should also be replaced and saved. Do not pack the vagina.

139. B: Air sounds in the epigastrium indicate that the tube has been incorrectly placed in the esophagus; the tube should then be removed and the process repeated. You may need to press on the patient's throat to view the vocal cords in order to maneuver the tube correctly. The tube should be held against the patient's teeth to ensure that it does not move. You may not necessarily need two hands to work the bag-valve-mask unit (BVM) because the patient will be less resistant to ventilation.

140. D: Activated charcoal is contraindicated in patients who have ingested acids or alkalis, such as those found in bathroom or oven cleaners, in patients who have ingested gasoline during siphoning, and in those with altered mental status.

141. B: Activated charcoal is the preferred line of treatment for a poisoning victim and is superior to syrup of ipecac in speed and effectiveness. Only a few antidotes exist for a relatively small number of poisons. Because sorbitol acts very quickly, it is not usually given for poisoning in most EMS situations.

142. C: The first step in treating a patient with a severe allergic reaction is to manage the patient's airway and breathing. Administer high-concentration oxygen; if the patient has difficulty breathing, provide artificial ventilation. If the patient exhibits signs of shock such as altered mental status and has a prescribed epinephrine auto-injector, you should consult medical direction and if advised, administer the epinephrine; if the patient shows signs of shock but has not been prescribed epinephrine, you should treat for shock and transport immediately.

143. A: In the case of a patient who has had an allergic reaction in the past but has not been prescribed epinephrine and exhibits signs of shock such as altered mental status, increased pulse, reduced blood pressure, and nausea or vomiting, you should treat for shock and transport immediately.

144. B: If the patient exhibits signs of shock and has been prescribed an epinephrine auto-injector, you should call medical direction and if advised, administer epinephrine. If the patient does not have the auto-injector with them, you may request an advanced life support (ALS) intercept; paramedics carry and can administer epinephrine.

145. A: Musculoskeletal injuries carry the risk of nerve and blood vessel injury; for this reason, you should assess distal pulse, motor function, and sensation (PMS) before splinting.

146. C: Patients with a painful, swollen, or deformed extremity should be treated for possible fracture. After assessing distal PMS, you should splint the wrist, then reassess. Check for nerve injury by asking the patient if he or she can move the injured part or feel your touch. Never induce crepitus, a grating sound or feeling that causes severe pain. Realignment is unnecessary unless the hand is cyanotic or lacks pulses.

147. A: A joint locked in a normal or abnormal position may be dislocated. Joint injuries should usually be splinted in the direction in which they were found; in the case of an angulated injury to the ulna, femur, or radius that cannot fit into a rigid splint, you should realign the bone.

148. A: A patient with an injury to the tibia or fibula should be treated for shock. Administer high-concentration oxygen and splint the injury. Do not apply manual traction, or tension, and do not apply an ice pack directly to the skin.

149. C: Concussion may result in amnesia, or short-term loss of memory of the events surrounding the accident; however, concussion rarely results in long-term memory loss.

150. D: In removing an injured child from a car safety seat, apply a cervical collar to maintain manual stabilization of the head and neck. Do not slide the child out of the seat or strap the child to the backboard across the abdomen. Taping the child across the chin may put pressure on the neck.

Made in the USA
Middletown, DE
15 May 2016